Praise for *AI-Human Fu...*

AI doesn't have to be cold, confusing or completely disconnected from reality and, thankfully, Leanne Shelton gets that. In *AI-Human Fusion*, she throws out the jargon and shows real people how to use AI with confidence, personality, and purpose. This isn't another hype-filled tech manual. It's a human-first, sanity-saving guide for leaders who want to explore AI without losing themselves or their audience along the way. Smart, grounded and extremely timely.

Andrew Griffiths, international bestselling author and global speaker

I've learned from countless experts on AI, and Leanne is unique among them, so I'm not surprised she produced such a singular book. *AI-Human Fusion* is what happens when a deeply curious and inquisitive – and highly practical – mind meets a subject that is too often discussed in the abstract. This is the guide to implementing AI in your business "for the rest of us" which I bet a lot of people have been waiting for.

Christopher Mims, technology journalist, *Wall Street Journal*

AI-Human Fusion couldn't have landed at a more critical time. We're navigating an era where the digital noise is deafening and the pressure to keep up is relentless. And yet, amidst all the hype and fear-mongering around AI, Leanne Shelton delivers something rare – a grounded, human-first guide that's as practical as it is powerful.

This book is the circuit breaker we didn't know we needed. It challenges the status quo and replaces overwhelm with opportunity. As someone deeply committed to helping women step into their brilliance, own their positioning, and build commercially smart businesses, I see *AI-Human Fusion* as essential reading. Leanne demystifies AI with clarity, courage, and charisma. She's not just teaching tools, she's empowering us to own our voice in an AI-driven world.

If you've ever felt intimidated by tech or worried you'd be left behind, this book is your invitation to lead the charge instead. Because the future isn't AI or human. It's both. And this is your permission slip to be unapologetically YOU while harnessing the power of what's next.

Janine Garner, mentor, bestselling author and rebel with a cause

You don't need to know how generative AI works, but you do need to learn how to use it to stay ahead in your career. Leanne Shelton – an early adopter and passionate advocate of the use of GenAI in the workplace – makes that case clearly, sharing how professionals can embrace AI in a way that enhances their unique values and skills, rather than replaces the need for them. Through her thoughtful insights, personal anecdotes and evident passion for traditional creativity, she shows how to understand AI simply – and integrate AI gently – in an authentic and unique way. If you are someone from a non-tech background wanting to know how to use AI to your advantage, this is a must-read.

Marty McCarthy, news editor, tech and innovation, LinkedIn

Learning how to use AI tools in line with my values and ethics has at times felt rather precarious. I wish I'd been able to read this book before I'd jumped headfirst into it all. I'd recommend it to anyone wanting to use AI to help them develop ideas, create content and communicate with the real world around them.

This book is the practical and grounded guide you need to help you find that balance of using AI in high impact ways, without feeling like you are selling your soul to do it.

I love that *AI-Human Fusion* reminds us that technology can amplify our ability to better connect with others rather than break it down. Leanne Shelton has done a magnificent job of helping us all find a way to use the tools before us intelligently, while keeping our integrity intact.

Rachel Klaver, prolific author, straight-up marketing strategist and trainer

*A non-techy,
human-first approach to AI
for busy leaders*

AI
HUMAN
FUSION

LEANNE SHELTON

MAJOR
STREET

MAJOR STREET

First published in 2025 by Major Street Publishing Pty Ltd
info@majorstreet.com.au | majorstreet.com.au

© Leanne Shelton 2025
The moral rights of the author have been asserted.

A catalogue record for this book is available
from the National Library of Australia

NATIONAL
LIBRARY
OF AUSTRALIA

Printed book ISBN: 978-1-923186-31-6
Ebook ISBN: 978-1-923186-32-3

Cover design by Typography Studio
Internal design by Production Works

10 9 8 7 6 5 4 3 2 1

Contents

Disclaimer

All information in this book was accurate at the time of publication. However, as details may change over time, readers are encouraged to refer to the accompanying online resources for the most up-to-date information or corrections relevant to the content presented in this publication.

You can access the *AI-Human Fusion* online resources via the QR code below:

humanedgeai.com/ai-human-fusion-resources

Foreword

In a world that's evolving faster than we can blink, artificial intelligence has emerged as one of the most transformative forces shaping our professional and personal lives. For many of us, the term 'AI' still carries an air of mystery. What impact will it have on our jobs? What about our personal lives? Often with things that are disruptive, we may pause with concern.

I initially met Leanne online in early 2024 and immediately felt her passion for the AI space. Rather than being caught up in the typical 'shininess' of the tools, she had a real human-centred approach that I was drawn towards. As someone with over 20 years' experience in leading multi-faceted learning teams, I could instantly see her potential. Leanne asked me to be her mentor, and I jumped onboard; however, I feel the learning experience has been a two-way street.

One thing I've learnt from Leanne is that now is not the time to pause but the time to act. If you're not engaging with AI today, then you risk being left behind tomorrow. Replacing your concern with curiosity is one of the key lessons to learn from this book. Actually, it's a great approach to any significant changes in life.

AI-Human Fusion offers a timely guide to understanding, embracing and applying the power of AI. Leanne delivers sought-after advice with down-to-earth storytelling, infused with her special brand of effervescence and humour. As a learning and development expert, I know this is vital when it comes to effective in-person facilitation and written explanations.

Leanne brings together two unique concepts of our time: the need to be authentically ourselves and the need to embrace and engage AI tools. So, how do you be yourself while engaging with AI tools? Leanne shares her wisdom on these concepts in this book – presenting a balanced approach to AI, demystifying technical jargon, introducing practical steps to train AI to sound like you, and engaging with AI in meaningful, human-centric ways. From developing a curious mindset, to thinking of it as a junior member of your team, to ensuring ethical and responsible use and embracing your audience, you *can* remain 'human-first' in an AI-driven world.

Leanne draws on her years of experience in copywriting and marketing to empower you to see AI as an assistant that can enhance your work, creativity and productivity. Whatever purpose you are looking to achieve with AI tools, there must be the human component. AI might speed us up, or simplify or provide us with working drafts, but nothing will replace that human connection, creativity and critical thinking. AI will help us skip the first few steps and give us the space to focus on what truly matters: our relationships, our values and our purpose.

In the chapters ahead, you'll discover how to integrate AI tools into your work in a way that enhances your authenticity, increases your productivity and prepares your team for the future. By the time you turn the last page, you'll have the tools and mindset necessary to embrace AI with the confidence to be yourself.

Welcome to the future, where AI meets humanity.

Mehri Doyle
Board Member, Australian Institute of Training and Development

Prologue

The HABITS Framework

If you were to travel back in time and tell any version of Leanne she'd be the author of a book on artificial intelligence one day, I can honestly say she'd laugh in your face:

> *Me? Writing a book about a "technical" subject as an AI thought-leader? Yeah, right. What's that? I'm also conducting keynotes and workshops about AI as my core business? Umm, sorry.*
> *I think you've got the wrong Leanne Shelton. Or maybe your brain is still a bit rattled from your trip in the time machine.*

However, it's all true – because here I am. I'm living proof that AI can create positive changes when you seek the opportunities, rather than freak out about the dystopian possibilities. While AI had a direct impact on the shrivelling up of my copywriting and content marketing business, I'm doing more than okay. After transitioning into the new and exciting role of Global AI Coach, I haven't felt the urge to look back.

Despite identifying myself as a writer my whole life, I simply never felt the same level of enthusiasm for copywriting as I do for AI. Sure, I enjoyed it immensely – especially when my agency was at its financial peak – but I didn't feel the need to constantly talk about the craft. In comparison, these days I struggle to stop the flood of AI insights and learnings from pouring out of me every time it pops up in conversation. (If you've been on the receiving end of these outbursts, #sorrynotsorry.) I just have so much to say, so much misuse to fight against and so many misunderstandings to put right.

This is why I've written *AI-Human Fusion*. I needed a platform to help busy leaders like yourself see AI for what it is: a tool to enhance our experience and expertise, not to replace us. I wanted to create a safe space to allow you to pause and truly understand this new accessible AI phenomenon, including where the humans fit in. There's just so much noise and hype out there, making it hard to rationally think things through. This is your opportunity to step back, learn and decide your path. This is my gift to you.

From SEO copywriting to AI coaching

If you've been following me for a while, you might be familiar with the story around my business pivot. For everyone else, let's briefly take a walk down memory lane.

Let me take you back to early 2023, when my nine-year-old copywriting and content marketing business, Write Time Marketing, saw a drop in conversions. It was partly due to the tough economic climate and partly due to the shiny, new and *free* competitor that had entered the scene: OpenAI's ChatGPT.

I admit my initial reaction was to freak out. My services were already undervalued in the small-business space, where low budgets ruled the roost. How could my agency possibly charge for writing services and marketing strategies when AI promised to do it all for free and within seconds? Basically, I had a choice: I could bury my head in the sand, rock in the corner, pull my hair out or engage in any other stress-related metaphor, or, instead of fighting my new competitor and losing, I could just accept that this was my new reality. I could accept that everyone would start using AI at some point, so I should embrace it and understand it.

With my writing background, I was understandably annoyed with the robotic, lifeless AI-generated content I'd started to see populating my social media feeds. I was also frustrated by every man and his dog jumping on the AI bandwagon, selling those massive prompt kits – like 1,000 prompts for $57 – that only focused on the input. None of these people (usually business coaches) were talking about what to do with the output produced or how to ensure it was well written and personalised prior to flicking it out into the world. And none of these people were discussing *how* these prompts could be effectively customised and applied by their followers. Out of curiosity, I purchased one of these guides and tested the prompts myself. In the majority of cases, the content produced was unusable, generic garbage.

In April 2023, at a quarterly planning event with a networking group, ChatGPT popped up in conversation. I shared my frustrations about the misuse of AI-generated content – and others shared their fears around using it. It was there that an idea formed in my imaginative, neurodiverse brain: what if I were to put together a webinar on AI from the perspective of a copywriter? I'd been running content marketing workshops on various topics for five years, including webinars, LinkedIn, business blogging, podcasts and website copy. Why not make ChatGPT my next training focus? I asked around the room and it was unanimous: everyone was keen to learn more.

Not one to procrastinate on big, exciting ideas, I set a date for a free webinar titled "How to use ChatGPT and still sound human" and gave myself a month to learn everything I could about the topic. (Nothing like a deadline, right?) There were literally three books on Amazon about ChatGPT at the time. Two of them were so poorly written, I couldn't get past the first few pages. The third was pretty good, opening my eyes to the concept of prompt engineering and how it works. I also listened to some AI podcasts. I admit imposter syndrome regularly showed its ugly head during this process. When it did, I just assured myself I was fine if I knew 10% more than the people in the virtual room.

By the time the webinar day rolled around, I'd collected 150 registrations, with 70 tuning in live. Not bad for my first attempt to educate others on AI. The feedback was extremely positive, and everything seemed to snowball from there. The next thing I knew, I was featured in *The Australian* newspaper, with a page-three article and my photo on the front page. Frequent requests to speak at conferences, summits and networking events quickly followed, including multiple visits to Kuala Lumpur, Malaysia, to run a series of two-day AI workshops.

Somewhere along the line, I realised I was onto something. Maybe AI training should be more than just a side project.

After all, with almost 20 years' experience in writing and marketing, I had an opportunity here to play to my strengths and help leaders create their own prompts that would lead to higher quality output. My bubbly personality and professional speaking and training skills (plus high-school drama classes) also gave me an engaging edge. Being a woman in the male-dominated tech industry didn't hurt either. So, I decided to officially make my mark in the positive, human-first AI movement by launching my new business, HumanEdge AI Training, in April 2024.

Why this book matters

Okay, Leanne, I have AI-Human Fusion *in my hands. But won't any type of AI education I learn today be completely out of date in a few months?*

Great question. The continual, fast-moving advancements of AI tools and technology in recent years made me hesitant about writing an AI-related book until now. I was concerned about releasing something that would need a whole chunk of adjustments only a month or two later, which was an issue experienced by my AI-author counterparts. But then I realised my message is so much bigger than the tools and technology itself, and I have an opportunity here to bring up thought-provoking concepts that others aren't questioning or talking about enough.

Unlike many AI enthusiasts, I'm not solely focused on the practical side of AI. I don't jump onto every new tool or update and constantly share new prompts to experiment with. However, I do continually reflect on how every new announcement could potentially affect humanity, and I see myself as having the important role of helping others see the updates for what they are: shiny distractions.

My aim for this book is to help busy leaders like you push through the noise and work out your place in this new AI-infused world we're now swimming in. You need to keep your human head above the water without allowing the AI tools to pull you under. I believe the real competitive edge for us as leaders comes from understanding how to think about AI – how to train it, critique it and use it strategically.

According to the Global AI Index published in September 2024, Australia was ranked 17th for AI capacity. Yep, we're way behind the eight-ball compared to countries like the USA (1st), the UK (4th), Germany (7th) and the Netherlands (13th). Apart from our small population size, I believe this ranking reflects our insecurities and uncertainties about completely embracing AI. There are just so many unknown factors sending many of us into a state of overwhelm. With a confused mind saying "no", it makes sense why the big organisations and networks I'm speaking to are populated by employees and business owners who are too scared to even touch AI, let alone integrate it into day-to-day tasks.

Let me assure you, AI will never replace you. AI will never completely take over humanity as we know it. But we do need to establish clear boundaries between where AI stops and human experience and expertise take over. Right now, we need to be focused on building our AI literacy – and that's not about chasing trends highlighted by the media and AI enthusiasts online. It's about developing the mindset and skills that will keep you at the forefront, no matter how AI evolves. It's about developing the perfect AI-human fusion of all the puzzle pieces at play.

While I started my AI journey by calling myself an "AI Trainer", during the past year I changed my title to "AI Coach". It seemed to be a better fit, because rather than telling leaders how to use AI, I'd much prefer to guide you towards the best solutions for your organisation. With AI, there are no absolutely correct answers. There is no one-size-fits-all approach. You need humans to make educated decisions about AI's place in your world.

This book matters because you deserve to be completely informed and organised when it comes to implementing AI in your company or business. Rather than being swept up in the excitement or pressured by increased productivity promises, taking the time to absorb the content within these pages will provide you with an educated, holistic view of it all. And you deserve that.

How this book will help you

If you were drawn to the words "non-techy" on the front cover, you can rest assured that this book is as non-technical as possible (if you haven't already gotten that vibe by my words so far). As well as sharing my own musings and learnings collected throughout my personal AI journey, I also feature insights and information from real-life humans in my network, including fellow leaders and experts on topics outside my expertise. You'll see these "Hear from the humans" extracts and quotes scattered throughout to add more depth to the AI conversation.

Overall, my aim is to take you from feeling unprepared, unclear and unskilled when it comes to AI to feeling prepared, purposeful and progressive, ultimately leading to greater productivity. Because "productivity" is usually the desired goal of utilising AI, right?

Introducing the AI-Human Fusion HABITS Framework

For an effective and human-first approach to AI, you need to apply a balanced fusion of four key aspects, which I refer to as HABITS. I believe this acronym is especially suitable because, in this fast-paced digital world we've found ourselves in, developing healthy AI habits is absolutely vital. Not to be too ominous too soon in the book, but our future depends on it.

This framework will help guide your journey of understanding throughout the book:

- **H - Humans:** prioritising a human-first approach by overcoming overwhelm, embracing AI without fear and maintaining strong human connections in an AI-driven world.
- **A - AI:** understanding how to train and implement AI effectively, covering both internal (operations, workflows) and external (customer engagement, marketing) applications.
- **BI - Business Integration:** embedding AI into business structures responsibly, including AI policy, cybersecurity, privacy, ethics and governance.
- **TS - Tactical Strategy:** developing practical, action-oriented approaches for integrating AI within your team, combining short-term implementation tactics with long-term strategic vision.

By following the framework, you'll achieve a holistic, human-first AI approach that will help produce positive and responsible outcomes. I've included actionable activities and links to online resources throughout the book for further support. But please don't let your AI literacy stop at the last page. With the AI world continually changing, there are bound to be updates. On that note: while everything featured within this book was correct at time of publication, you can keep across potential changes via the QR code below, which takes you to a webpage highlighting new information.

In the meantime, I hope *AI-Human Fusion* leaves you in a state of educated enlightenment – and that you enjoy reading it as much as I enjoyed writing it.

Remember to keep it human,

Leanne Shelton
February 2025

Glossary
(aka the "Techy Stuff")

Ugh, the techy stuff? Are you serious, Leanne? I picked up this book because I was drawn to the cover, which said "a non-techy human-first approach to AI for busy leaders". I'm not a technical person. That stuff scares me. Overwhelms me. Bores me. Do I really need to read this glossary, or can I skip over it?

Okay, I'm going to be absolutely honest here: I wanted to write this glossary just as much as you want to read it. I don't have a background in IT – and technology and I don't always get along. (Just ask my husband…)

My dislike for the techy stuff is reflected by most people I run AI training with. Most of them don't want to know about the nitty gritty, behind-the-scenes stuff about this newfangled technology taking over the planet. They just want to know the parts of AI that are relevant to them so they can start exploring, experimenting and effectively applying it to enhance their own and their team's daily productivity ASAP. Since you're reading this book, I assume you feel the same way. The reality is that I simply couldn't write a book about AI without defining at least some of the typical terms you'll hear regularly uttered by your IT team or more AI-savvy counterparts. I'd be doing you a disservice otherwise – and that's the last thing I want to do. So, I've pulled together a list of core definitions. Feel free to dog-ear this glossary as a quick reference whenever an AI term comes up in conversation. It will help you feel less lost and more intelligent. You're welcome!

Key AI Terms to Know

Artificial Intelligence

The term "artificial intelligence", or AI, was first coined in 1956 by computer scientist John McCarthy during the Dartmouth conference – an event which allegedly ignited the idea of AI as a scientific field.

AI refers to **the simulation of human intelligence in machines programmed to think and learn**. The systems are designed to perform tasks typically requiring human intelligence, such as analysing data, recognising speech and making predictions.

Today, AI is becoming a cornerstone of digital transformation across industries – driving innovation, improving efficiencies and enabling new business models. (But you're probably already aware of that part!)

Machine learning

Machine learning (ML) is **a part of AI that allows computers to learn and improve from experience instead of following fixed rules**. It works by analysing data to find patterns, make predictions or get better at tasks over time.

For example, ML can help a system predict what a customer might want to buy based on their past shopping habits. It can also be used to spot fraudulent activity, suggest personalised products or plan maintenance before problems occur. ML has become a key tool for businesses looking to work smarter and make better decisions.

Natural language processing

Natural language processing (NLP) refers to **the way AI understands and works with human language**. It's what allows computers to analyse, interpret and respond to text or speech.

From chatbots answering customer queries to tools that translate languages, NLP powers many everyday applications. NLP can help make communication more efficient for businesses by automating responses or gaining insights from customer feedback. It's what makes AI feel a little more human.

Large language models

A large language model (LLM) is **a specific type of AI designed to understand and generate human-like text based on patterns in language**. Trained on large amounts of text data, LLMs focus on interpreting and responding to text inputs in a coherent and contextually relevant way. They serve as the foundation for tools like OpenAI's ChatGPT, Microsoft's Copilot and Google's Gemini.

While LLMs are often used for generating content, such as emails or chat responses, their primary role is language comprehension and interaction. They excel at tasks like drafting, summarising or translating text, making them invaluable for communication-heavy tasks.

It's important to note that while all generative AI tools that produce text are powered by LLMs, **not all LLMs are used exclusively for generative purposes**. Businesses can also leverage LLMs for automating workflows, improving customer support and enhancing operational efficiency by enabling seamless, human-like communication.

Generative AI

Generative AI (GenAI) is **a broader category of AI focused on creating new and original content, such as text, images, music, videos or code**. Unlike LLMs, which are specifically trained for text-based language understanding and interaction, GenAI encompasses a wide range of technologies capable of producing creative outputs across multiple mediums. For example, GenAI tools like ChatGPT, Copilot and Gemini provide text-based output, tools like DALL-E and Leonardo.Ai create images, and Jukebox and Suno create music.

GenAI stands out for its ability to create unique and innovative content, giving businesses new ways to develop ideas, solve problems and design products.

ChatGPT

Developed by OpenAI and launched in November 2022, Chat Generative Pre-trained Transformer (ChatGPT) was the first widely accessible tool showcasing the power of GenAI in a conversational format. It **allows users to interact with AI in natural, human-like dialogue**, making it invaluable for tasks like drafting reports, brainstorming ideas and answering complex questions.

As part of the broader GenAI family, which also includes tools like Copilot and Gemini, ChatGPT highlights the potential of AI to transform how we work and communicate. Businesses can use ChatGPT to save time, increase efficiency and explore creative solutions, setting the stage for a future where GenAI becomes a trusted collaborator across industries.

Prompt engineering

Prompt engineering is **the skill of writing clear and specific instructions to get the best results from AI tools**.

A good prompt tells the AI tool exactly what you need, such as a thorough marketing plan or the answer to a tricky question. This skill is becoming essential for businesses using AI, as it bridges the gap between the technology's potential and practical, real-world results. Humans within businesses need to know how to ask the right questions to get the smartest answers.

Agentic AI

Agentic AI refers to **AI systems that can act on their own to complete tasks or solve problems without constant human guidance**. These systems don't need to wait for instructions because they can take initiative based on their goals. For example, a smart assistant that schedules meetings or adjusts priorities without being told is using agentic AI.

While this can boost productivity, it requires careful planning to ensure the system behaves responsibly and aligns with business needs. You also want to ensure a human expert always remains in control to train, manage and improve the set-up as required.

Retrieval-augmented generation

Retrieval-augmented generation (RAG) is **an AI method where tools like ChatGPT access external databases or sources to retrieve accurate and relevant information before generating a response.** Instead of relying solely on existing training data, RAG helps AI provide answers that are both current and context-specific.

Businesses often use RAG to enhance accuracy and credibility, especially in knowledge-intensive fields like law, medicine and finance. (Think of it like giving Chatty a research assistant to fetch reliable facts before she answers!)

AI hallucinations

In AI, "hallucinations" refer to situations when tools like ChatGPT generate responses that sound convincing but are incorrect or entirely made up. These inaccuracies occur because the AI generates answers based on patterns, not verified facts, sometimes leading it confidently astray. For businesses, managing hallucinations involves careful training, clear prompting and fact-checking. Keeping humans involved ensures accuracy stays front and centre!

Final thoughts...

How are you feeling after reading through those definitions? Is everything starting to make sense?

If you're still feeling a bit clueless, that's okay. You can always turn to your GenAI tool and write or verbalise the prompt, "Could you please explain [insert AI term here] in a simple way that a

12-year-old would understand?" Then, continue to ask questions until you have that sudden a-ha moment. For example:

Leanne's input:

> *Could you please explain Natural Language Processing in a simple way that a 12-year-old would understand?*

ChatGPT output (unedited):

> *Sure! Imagine you're talking to a robot, and you want it to understand what you're saying—just like a friend would. **Natural Language Processing (NLP)** is the special technology that helps computers understand, read, and even talk in human language.*

Think of it like this:

- *__Words and Sentences:__ Just like we learn words and how to put them into sentences, computers need to learn that too!*
- *__Understanding Meaning:__ Computers don't naturally "get" jokes, feelings, or double meanings, so NLP helps them figure out what words really mean in different situations.*
- *__Talking Back:__ When you ask Siri or Alexa a question, NLP helps them understand what you mean and give you the right answer.*

> *It's like teaching a pet parrot, but instead of just copying words, the computer actually learns what they mean!* ☺

Bit of fun, right? Honestly, you can still embrace AI without diving too deeply into these definitions or memorising anything. I promise there won't be a quiz at the end of the book!

PART I

HUMANS

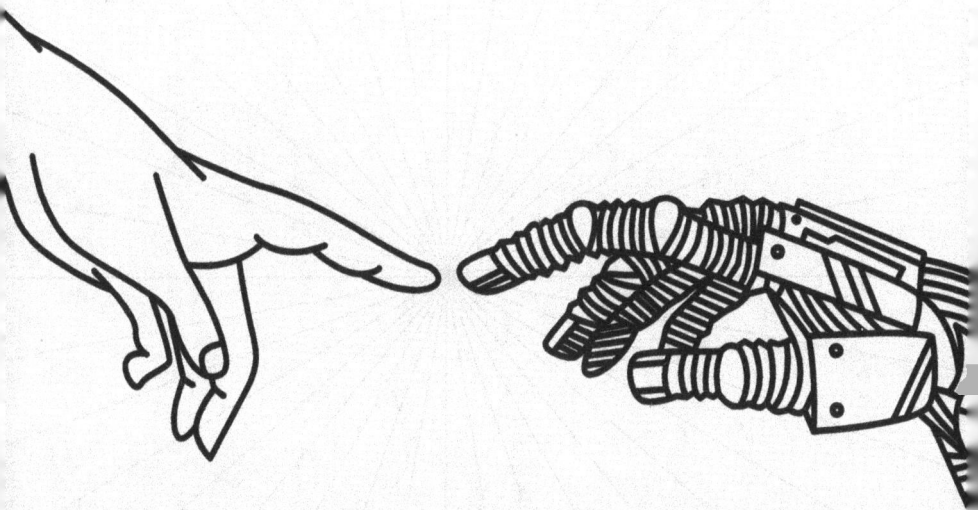

Chapter 1

Let's Press Pause

"People are trying to work out how to harness AI to ensure
their business maintains a point of difference ... But how
can we stay at the forefront of something moving so quickly,
without becoming a 'me-too' brand/follower?"

Rachel McIver

Right now, many of us are scared about the unknown world of
AI, but I know we'll be okay. This isn't the first time humanity has
encountered a new invention entering the market. It's happened
many times before. While some people saw them as passing fads
not to be concerned with, others became paranoid about the
world ending. History is simply repeating itself with the release of
accessible GenAI.

Guess what? Whatever the perspective, humanity has somehow
survived. Sure, there were some inventions that led to injury or
death. *(Wow, Leanne, that took a sudden dark turn...)* But in most
cases, humans found a way to accept or adapt to the new change.

I'm here to tell you that we *will* get through the scary, unknown
aspects of AI and where it could take us in the future. It's just
somewhat difficult to see the forest for the trees.

As a fun little exercise, I've pulled together a list of retrospectively amusing quotes from people and publications about new inventions causing chaos throughout history:

- **1876 – Telephone:** Someone from one of the USA's largest telecom companies, Western Union, allegedly wrote an internal memo that said, "This 'telephone' has too many shortcomings to be seriously considered as a means of communication. The device is inherently of no value to us".

- **1879 – Lightbulb:** Henry Morton, President of the Stevens Institute of Technology, said, "Anyone who is familiar with it will recognise that Mr. Edison's light bulb is a clear failure".

- **1899 – Cars:** The *Literary Digest* magazine said, "The ordinary 'horseless carriage' is at present a luxury for the wealthy, and although its price will fall in the future, it will never come into as common use as the bicycle".

- **1928 – Talkies:** When sound films were first exhibited, Joseph Schenck, President of United Artists, told *The New York Times*, "Talking doesn't belong in pictures … I don't think people will want talking pictures long".

- **1946 – Television:** Film producer, Darryl Zanuck said, "People will soon get tired of staring at a plywood box every night".

- **1977 – Home computers:** Ken Olsen, founder of computer company Digital Equipment Corp, said, "There is no reason anyone would want a computer in their home".

- **1985 – Laptops:** A journalist from *The New York Times* said, "The limitations come from what people actually do with computers, as opposed to what the marketers expect them to do. On the whole, people don't want to lug a computer with them to the beach or on a train to while away hours. They would rather spend time reading the sports or business section of the newspaper. Somehow, the microcomputer industry has assumed that everyone would love to have a keyboard grafted on as an extension of their fingers. It just is not so".

Rachel McIver, CEO and Principal Consultant at azura people, had some really interesting insights to add about email and sustainability practices:

> *Take the example of when the world of email and the paperless office was first talked about many decades ago. They predicted people would have more leisure time and that cities would need to be redesigned around leisure facilities because people would be working less. What happened? We just accepted the productivity gains for the workplace, instead of the worker, and produced more.*

It looks like similar predictions are being made now. Someone made a comment to me recently that they predict AI will replace all our jobs by 2030, so we'll be all out playing golf every day. Apart from the fact that I have a terrible swing and could never see myself playing golf day in, day out, I doubt that's what our lives will become. (Unless that's your lifestyle by choice, of course!)

You've probably seen your fair share of negative, fear-mongering quotes about AI from influential leaders or tabloid publications as well. In 50 years, I'm sure people will look back on how we're feeling right now and laugh. Thinking about the bigger picture, you could compare current times with the start of the industrial revolution around 1760. According to the history books, that caused a "slight" change to society as we know it. But we made it work. Humanity is probably well overdue for a similar shake-up!

Freaking out about AI?

AI is here. It's accessible. And it's apparently super easy to implement. But the fast-paced changes and constant talk about future possibilities of what's coming up next are bloody scary.

You're caught up in the whirlwind of what-ifs. And you're feeling the pressure to embrace *all* the tools and see instant improvements on productivity levels and the bottom line. Somehow, it feels hard to get your head around it all. And you can't stop procrastinating. You feel out of touch because you've only logged into ChatGPT a few times, while colleagues are building armies of AI agents.

The thing is, while it's been around for decades, AI feels new to most people. And overwhelming. There are just so many elements to think about, like data security, prompt engineering, ethical usage, maintaining human connection and ensuring quality. And you don't want to get it wrong.

Look, I know it's a lot. But if it's any comfort to you, there's no need to have all the answers and experiment with everything at once. Sometimes you're better off delegating tasks to a team member rather than spending hours trying to figure out a tool yourself. I'm here to assure you we're *all* on this journey of exploration, because nobody knows how things will evolve in the future. Even my fellow AI enthusiasts and trainers admit to experiencing massive imposter syndrome. We've all found ourselves guiding people through an uncertain technological age with advancements moving quicker than the speed of light. We definitely feel the pressure to keep up with it all. So, I totally get you.

The best way to approach AI is to consider how it fits into the big picture within your team and business. Rather than embracing 101 AI tools at once, wasting precious time in the exploration process, you could start with one simple option that fulfills a need within one simple daily task. Rather than adding the fuel to the fire and freaking out about potential AI-induced redundancies, you could set aside a little bit of time every week to find ways to upskill via trustworthy resources and training.

With this book in your hands, you have a golden tool to move through all the core aspects you *need* to know about AI. Just trust the process, and you'll feel more confident about AI by the final pages.

In this chapter, I address some of those elephants in the room and help you slow down the tornado (or tornadoes!) spinning within your brain.

Why AI feels overwhelming

With new tools and tech constantly flooding our feeds, it's no wonder we feel stuck in a love–hate relationship with AI. One minute we're intrigued by what it can do, and the next we're googling "Will AI replace me?" (Spoiler alert: it won't if you don't allow it.)

The truth is, AI isn't here to outshine our human brilliance. I strongly believe it's here to support it. But first, you need to move past the fear and confusion to see it for what it really is: *a tool to help you work smarter, not harder.* Sure, most of these tools look intimidating to the non-techy brain at first. But once you know how to use them correctly and efficiently (or ignore them completely), there's the potential to feel both powerful and productive.

One of the core concerns I hear is the fear of being left behind or replaced: "If I don't learn about all this AI stuff now and become really good at it, what will happen to me in my role/business?"

The pressure to jump onboard the AI train can then lead to anxiety, especially for 'older' individuals and those who feel they lack the technical expertise. This anxiety transforms into procrastination, which leads to guilt or irritation with oneself. Sound familiar? If yes, I urge you to be kind to yourself and just start taking baby steps. Allow yourself to absorb the concepts in Part I: Humans, before continuing with the rest of the book. You've got this!

We've all got so much sh*t going on

Putting AI in the corner for a moment, I recognise there are likely to be various other things going on in your professional life that are contributing to your sense of overwhelm. AI adaptation is just one in a long list of stressors in the mix.

The Gartner report *Top 5 priorities for HR leaders in 2025* highlights that 75% of HR leaders believe their managers are overwhelmed by the expanding scope of their responsibilities. You know, like embracing technology that's always been dealt with by the IT team in the past.

As a leader you might feel the same way – like *everything* falls onto you to get right. And that equals overwhelm. Unfortunately, I think misuse of AI will add to this issue – especially if people start to hand over *all* their thinking to the bots, making it harder to think strategically, critically or creatively for themselves. This is another reason why we need to be wary of the habits we establish with these tools. (This is where my 'human-first' approach comes in, which we'll review in the following chapters.)

The report also indicates that 73% of HR leaders believe employees are fatigued by change. That is *not* a good sign considering we've entered the digital age of AI, where the technology is advancing quicker than you can say, "Change is inevitable". It's even more concerning that 74% say their managers aren't equipped to lead the change either. From personal experience, I know how hard it is to embrace change effectively when burnt out. So, the last thing you need as a burnt-out leader is pressure to success-fully lead your burnt-out team through the unknown terrains of AI.

If it makes you feel any better, the Gartner report highlights that the key to creating sustainable change is to have it be "led from within the organisation". So, now is not the time to act like a martyr or bury your head in the sand. Be open to the idea of getting your whole team onboard and exploring the world of AI together. I talk more about the best practices to smoothly introduce your team to AI in Chapter 14: Building an AI-ready Team Culture. Ultimately, both you and your team need to feel in control, without job risk, to ensure a positive future.

In addition to the professional pressures, you're likely to have other sh*t going on in your life, like managing your health, partner, kids, ageing parents, sick pets and general financial issues. You could ask AI for guidance on some of those aspects. Just remain vigilant, and please don't accept what it spits out as gospel. There are plenty of human experts out there who are much better equipped to offer support. While I'm not a qualified expert in those areas (although I could share a bunch of life lessons as a wife and mother!), I *can* help you deal with the AI stuff.

We're worried AI will replace our jobs

Paranoid about being made redundant? Ah, this misconception is a classic – and a favourite among the fear-mongering media. But I don't believe it's true.

Well, not completely.

With the invention of social media, the internet, electricity and other technological advancements, most jobs haven't disappeared. However, they *have* evolved. We still have bank tellers and account-ants, even though we now have ATMs and accounting software; their roles have simply become more advisory. And we still have marketing professionals and graphic designers, even though we're all capable of doing our own emails and socials thanks to tools like Canva. They're the experts we turn to for big campaigns and projects. We also still have sales representatives and customer service teams, even though things can be automated via robotic messages and chatbots, because a lot of the time we still want to talk to a *human*!

You get the picture. We need to be prepared for our roles to change in the near future, whatever that may look like. Upskilling in AI, rather than ignoring it, will ensure your employability to some level.

Hey, I'm speaking from experience here. I am a human copywriter who still has a place in this world. But rather than having businesses turn to me to write content for them (aka a done-for-you approach), I've taken on an advisory role to help them write high-quality content with AI (a done-with-you approach). For any struggling copywriters reading this, I highly recommend getting a firm grasp of prompt engineering basics so you can help others as well (as highlighted in Chapter 4: Prompt Engineering 101) because you can't undervalue the amazing skillset you have. We bring something to the table that all the non-writers can't deliver.

Whatever your role, try to remain positive about the opportunities AI brings. As a positive thinker who has attracted countless opportunities in the past, I can honestly say you never know what's around the corner when you maintain a healthy mindset.

Hear from the humans
Sharona Radovsky, Specialist UX/SEO copywriter

My brother, who works at Google in the USA, first told me about AI when he was on a holiday in Australia around 2.5 years ago. He said, "Either get on board or get left behind. Copywriters who adopt AI will be the ones with jobs".

So, instead of sticking my head in the sand, I decided to be an early adopter. I explored every type of LLM I could get my hands on, testing them with various questions for days, weeks and months on end. I now use AI in my SEO copywriting role at a digital marketing company. Our clients are aware that I use it and they are very grateful for the quality writing.

Before AI came around, I was paid a large per-project fee as the senior UX/SEO copywriter. I was hired to write fully keyword-researched website content, SEO blog posts, e-books, sales landing pages, etc. Now, I work with AI on an hourly rate to generate as much SEO-optimised content as possible. An article that used to take me eight hours now takes me two, so I get through a lot more. I conduct competitor analysis and keyword research and then prompt AI with the information, including feeding it my own style guide. I then get it to generate an article outline and next get it to write the article. Once it's done to my standard, without any missing sections, and it flows nicely for the reader, I proofread and copy edit it to make sure it's perfect. The most important thing is that it's user friendly, well written and adds value. I have high standards, so I always ensure it does.

I don't know what the future of copywriting is, but at this stage, human-edited AI seems to be a growing sector. But then, everything could change within one to five years anyway, so these days I just take it a day at a time and live life more in the now.

We feel we need to have *all* the tools

If your newsfeed is anything like mine, you're probably constantly flooded with tools and messaging related to the AI world such as:

Use this tool, not that one.
Do this, don't do that.
Move across to this one, abandon that one.

The thing is, there are more than 18,000 AI tools in the world. Some have been produced as the result of extensive research, experimentation and financial investment; others have been developed by bored teenagers in their bedrooms late at night. Actually, probably 80% of them fall into that last category. Maybe more.

Just remember, a lot of these tools piggyback on the ChatGPT engine anyway. And in many cases, the LLM or GenAI you're currently experimenting with has all the functionality you *really* need.

When it comes to AI, one size doesn't fit all. The key to overcoming overwhelm is focusing on tools that align with your unique needs and goals, rather than trying to master everything out there. Don't let yourself get caught up in the trends and invest heavily in a dozen of them, especially when some tools mightn't even exist in six months' time (or less)!

According to the Gartner survey *2024 Generative AI Planning*, 77% of respondents said AI tools have actually decreased their productivity and added to their workload. I think it's because people are finding themselves down the rabbit hole of wading through all the tools or trying to work out the best ways to use them. The fact is, the majority of tools are still in their infancy and probably require way too much human insight for quality assurance to make them worthwhile.

You know what? I actually only use a few tools myself. And they serve me well. I don't want to let myself get caught up in shiny AI tool syndrome and lose hours exploring and experimenting to find a way to be productive. Ironic, no? Sourcing and understanding AI tools is literally a full-time job for some people out there. It could potentially become a common job role one day!

I've come across many tools that are apparently amazing but have just led to disappointment and a waste of time. I'll share a funny story about this shortly.

At the time of writing, my core tools are ChatGPT (because it just knows me so well after more than two years of collaboration) and Otter.ai (for transcribing). I dabble in other tools from time to time and have heard great things about video editing tools, but I like working with Johan, my human video editor in the Philippines, and I trust his ability and decisions way more than a tool. I also feel good knowing I'm supplying work and money to another human rather than contributing to the "job replacement" saga.

According to the same Gartner report, 47% of employees using AI say they have no idea how to achieve expected productivity gains. This means the majority are simply fumbling their way through using the AI tools without a clue what they're doing. They're just told "Use these tools and be more productive" from higher up the food chain – without any clear direction. This is where AI team training comes in. (Hint: I *might* just know someone who could help in that area...)

I recommend thinking about what type of tools would make your life or work easier – saving time, sparking creativity or managing repetitive tasks – and start there.

For example, if you're juggling a million ideas, a tool like ChatGPT can help you brainstorm or structure your thoughts. If you need to pull together a webinar or pitch, Gamma's handy auto-populated, pretty presentation slides might be the perfect fit. Have a long meeting to sit through? Tools like Otter.ai can transcribe meetings so you can focus on the conversation, not note-taking.

The trick is to start with just one or two tools. Experiment, see what feels intuitive, and don't be afraid to abandon tools that don't click. If you need to pay, I suggest signing up for a month-by-month subscription. Then you can easily track and reflect on which tools you're actually using. Otherwise, you might "save money" signing up for 12 months but end up only using it for the first two weeks.

Hear from the humans
Mike Knapp, Software Engineer at Mottle

I'm conflicted. On one hand, AI is boosting productivity and opening doors to powerful new tools. On the other hand, it's also ushering in a surge of "noise" – including poorly conceived apps, content churned out for clicks, and superficial user experiences.

Given that our collective attention spans are already under stress, the increasing volume of low-value information is a concern.

A bigger risk is the possibility that today's "junk" transforms into tomorrow's hyper-personalised entertainment. Imagine Instagram reels tailored so precisely to each user's preferences that people stay "plugged in" for days. This scenario, reminiscent of a Matrix-style existence, no longer feels far-fetched.

We're confused by which "experts" to follow

When I decided to pivot into this new technological training space, I started following everyone on LinkedIn who had 'AI' mentioned in their profile byline. But those two letters don't instantly make them experts. As I've developed stronger and stronger opinions about ways you should and shouldn't use and view AI, I've started to become more and more critical when reading these people's posts or watching their videos about tools they recommend.

I have an amusing story to share about a situation when I experimented with an AI tool for the first time for a live, face-to-face team training session. I'd read great things about the tool that morning from an AI expert and was intrigued. I won't name and shame it, but the concept was that you could simply insert your company website URL into the tool and it would auto-populate a handful of social media graphics for you. Sounds cool, right?

So, I followed that exact process in front of the team and burst out laughing. One of the images produced featured the muscular upper body of a man in a navy business shirt with both hands out in "presentation mode". Now, I identify as a woman and my website features multiple photographs of me, so I don't know how it made that mistake. But that wasn't the funny part. The funny part was that the person had *no head*! Yep, it was the Headless Presenter. So. Dodgy.

The results from this experiment actually served me and my training session very well, because, as mentioned earlier, it highlighted my reasons for keeping my AI tool count to a minimum. Another point to me.

We're concerned about AI replacing our creativity and critical thinking skills

I classify myself as a creative woman. I completed a Bachelor of Creative Arts at Macquarie University, majoring in Creative Writing; I studied drama at school; and I have enjoyed dancing my whole life. I'm also the eldest daughter of a retired creative arts head teacher who specialised in visual arts. (While Dad is incredibly talented in that space, unfortunately I didn't inherit his clever drawing and painting skills ☹.) However, I believe being dragged to countless art exhibitions as a child and encouraged to think about every artist's intention for every piece (even when looking at random paint splatters on a canvas) helped fuel my outside-the-box thinking and creative entrepreneurial spirit.

So, yeah, I'm creative. Give me the opportunity to use my right brain any day over number-crunching statistics.

I'm also a critical thinker. And that's come in handy when running businesses for the past decade. Because rather than rocking in a corner and freaking out every time a problem popped up (you know, like when ChatGPT came out of nowhere and threatened my whole livelihood), I've jumped onto it and worked out the best steps forward.

I enjoy being creative. I enjoy putting on my thinking cap. I don't ever want AI to replace those things. They're part of my personality. But, I can use AI as a tool to support me. I regularly come across other creative leaders – including photographers, artists and videographers – who are worried about AI replacing their creativity and knowledge, but I always assure these artsy folk there's an opportunity here to use their expertise to make AI work *for* them. But only if they want to. Because there will *always* be humans out there who want to buy creations produced by humans. And if these creative geniuses are one day in the minority, that's a great opportunity to increase their prices!

AI is extremely useful for helping me push through procrastination. It removes that barrier to entry, enabling me to get started on a project when I'm otherwise feeling overwhelmed or brain dead. And you know what? Every time ChatGPT helps me kickstart the process, I get this amazing dose of dopamine:

> *Look at that instant output!*
> *Look at those ideas!*
> *Look at that structure!*

You know the enlightened sensation I'm talking about. The problem is, the majority of people stop there. In that initial moment of excitement, they go ahead and run with the very first thing AI pumps out without any analysis, without checking if the brand voice is any good and without critiquing the output.

But this initial stage should only be seen as the *beginning* of the creative process, not a replacement for it. This dopamine hit should simply lift that barrier to entry and fuel your creative and critical thinking process. *Then* you can use your experience and expertise to create some real magic. *Then* you can expand on those plans and strategies. *Then* you can challenge and critique what AI gives you and decide whether you continue with prompts or take over the project manually.

Rather than using up your creative juices on that white screen of death, you can preserve your creativity and have much more fun diving into projects where you can truly shine. The overarching message here? AI will only replace our creative and critical thinking if we let it.

Hear from the humans
Jamie van Leeuwen, Creative Director at Absolutely AI

I can understand the trepidation that many of you feel around the influx of AI – and the speed at which it is advancing. Within one year of image generators becoming mainstream, there were already more AI images generated than every photograph that has ever been taken in history – which is absolutely bonkers.

There will be job losses, I'm sure. But there'll be jobs created out of it too.

AI is an incredible tool, but it's just that – a tool. The real magic happens when someone with a vision and a story uses AI to bring it to life. If you have knowledge of a particular creative industry, you can use AI to enhance that. Some of the photography clubs I've been talking to don't want to generate anything with artificial intelligence, but they would like to know how they can add de-noising to their photographs, to upscale them using AI, to sharpen them using AI. There are ways that you can greatly enhance your current work using AI without altering the pixels.

AI can make creation faster and more affordable, but the heart and soul of storytelling will always come from us. I encourage creators to invest time in studying storytelling fundamentals – artistic movements, emotional triggers, and psychology – before diving into the tools.

Final thoughts...

AI doesn't have to be overwhelming, mysterious or intimidating. You just need to take a step back, break it all down and approach it with curiosity. The key is to remember you're in control. Don't get caught up in the hype. And go at your own pace.

Everyone is exploring and learning right now. And even if it looks from afar like someone is absolutely nailing the AI stuff, you don't always know the full story. You don't know how many sleepless nights went into it behind the scenes, or how many virtual assistants they have onboard doing all the grunt work.

You also don't know if their AI practices are creating the desired results – or how many humans are being neglected in the process.

AI-generated chapter summary *(with human tweaks)*

- Technological advancements often trigger fear and scepticism, but history shows that humans adapt and thrive.
- The rapid evolution of AI has created pressure to keep up, leading to anxiety, procrastination and self-doubt.
- AI is a tool, not a replacement – success lies in using it to enhance human expertise, not replace it.
- The fear of job loss due to AI mirrors past concerns about automation, but roles tend to evolve rather than disappear.
- AI overwhelm is real – there are thousands of tools, but mastering all of them is neither necessary nor productive.
- Strategic AI adoption means focusing on tools that genuinely support your work rather than chasing trends.
- Creativity and critical thinking remain essential – AI should be a starting point, not the final product.
- The key to navigating AI confidently is to take a step back, explore at your own pace and focus on purposeful implementation.

Chapter 2

The Importance of
Human Connection

*"Human connection isn't a luxury.
It's a necessity and core to being human."*

Kerryn Powell

When I started my content marketing business back in 2014, I had no idea what I was doing – like most new business owners. Apparently, there wasn't a "business manual" that I could follow to achieve success. Say what?

None of my family members or friends had been ignited by the entrepreneurial spark like me. At the time, I had a one-year-old daughter and we'd just moved to a new neighbourhood. All my close friends were either recent colleagues or mums from Playgroup. They. Did. Not. Get. It. They were either happily employed full-time or part-time, or stay-at-home mums. Ah, sometimes I wish my neurodiverse brain would be happy with that. I mean, why would *anyone* want to constantly hustle to make money when there's an option to remove the pressure and take home a reliable pay cheque?

Yes, we entrepreneurs are all a little insane (or neurodiverse), but we love it. Otherwise, we wouldn't do it. Anyway, if you're an entrepreneur like me, I'm sure you'd agree it can be an extremely lonely journey. That's why I looked into local face-to-face networking groups or masterminds in the early days, so I could surround myself with like-minded individuals. My fellow business owners have become my lifeline – and besties – over the past decade!

While I admit to attending networking events initially with the aim of drumming up work, I quickly discovered that these humans could offer me so much more. Over the years, I've received endless advice, encouragement and inspiration from them. These humans have become my biggest cheerleaders, referring and recommending me left, right and centre, both online and offline, and vice versa.

Okay, Leanne, what's the point of your story? What's it got to do with AI?

Well, thanks to networking, I've established and maintained a strong sense of human connection throughout the rollercoaster of entrepreneurial life. And for those of you employed, you've probably developed similar connections with some of your colleagues. There's nothing better than sharing frustrations and wins over lunch or after-work drinks. Especially when your partner, child, dog, cat or beloved pot plant at home doesn't fully understand what you're going through.

For me, the human connections I've built have proved valuable every time I've felt uncertain about business decisions and the world around me, or whenever I've had wins to celebrate. It's so much easier to enjoy your achievements when you have others cheering you on. These connections have also become the backbone of my social life and sparked numerous insightful conversations and laughter.

AI can't do all that.

Why we must "keep it human"

You've probably heard this countless times before, but humans have been "programmed" to crave connection and a sense of belonging. Back in the caveman days, we needed to be part of a tribe to ensure our survival. We needed to have someone keeping an eye out for wild animals while the rest of the tribe slept soundly. Some hunted for food while others nurtured the children. We relied on others for our safety and to keep uncertainty at bay.

Even though you're (highly) unlikely to bump into a sabre-toothed tiger in the modern world, the need for safety and security is still ingrained in us all. By default, as humans, we feel the need to prepare ourselves for any possible danger ahead. For some, this need manifests as massive anxiety. According to a 2020 to 2022 study by the Australian Bureau of Statistics, more than one in six Australians (17.2%, or 3.4 million people) aged between 16 and 85 years have had a 12-month anxiety disorder. That's a *lot* of people freaking out about stuff that *might* happen.

In a business context, the stats are even scarier. The 2024 ADP Research report *People at Work: A Global Workforce Review* highlights that Australians experience stress 12 times per week, making Australia the highest-rated country for stress in the Asia-Pacific. All this anxiety and stress isn't helped by the unknown world of AI, where job security and the pressure to conform to new technology has sent so many spiralling into overwhelm.

Right now, with AI capabilities getting stronger and stronger, we're all trying to predict and prepare for possible dangers ahead. But since none of us has dealt with this exact scenario before – and there's no real Dr Emmett Brown with a time machine to help us out – it's easy to get caught up in a complete freak-out zone, as addressed in the last chapter.

So, how do you push through this freak-out?

Well, you're reading these words right now because you're seeking advice from a fellow human, right? And you've probably watched AI enthusiasts* share tips on YouTube or TikTok, speak onstage, and post on LinkedIn. Me too. Because we're all looking for humans to provide us assurance, offer advice and tell us the best steps to take. We need to feel safe when we make mistakes and be guided towards solutions. We're basically looking for trusted experts to assure us everything is going to be all right – "There, there, darling. You'll get through this."

Artificial intelligence can't do all that. Especially when it's the problem.

So, in a confusing, ever-evolving AI space, we can't underestimate the power of human connection to make us feel safe.

Craving connection during COVID-19

I'm going to interrupt my own chapter here with musings around the "C-word": COVID-19. (I'll keep the swear words to a minimum, I promise!) I want to remind you of something important about human connection that you might've forgotten.

Everyone who found themselves cooped up within their own homes for extensive lockdown periods (#lockdowntrauma) during those "unprecedented times" experienced a major sense of disconnection from the world. And that had a dramatic impact on our mental health. The Australian Institute of Health and Welfare reports that nearly 17.6 million mental health-related services, subsidised by Medicare, were processed between 16 March 2020

---

* Just remember, you can't trust everything shared by AI enthusiasts. I recommend following lots of people and conducting some of your own research to become completely informed.

and 27 June 2021. Back then, we weren't mentally healthy people. And it makes sense.

What happens when someone tells you you're "not allowed" to meet and see other humans? You crave human connection even more. (Think of your rebellious teenage years when your parents told you not to date that "bad" boy or girl. It made you even more keen to sneak out to meet them, right?) Yes, even the introverts, who were initially thrilled about hanging out on the couch in their old underwear and holey shirts all day, requested FaceTime or Zoom chats with loved ones from time to time.

As humans, we're not programmed to be by ourselves. Just the other day, my family and I watched the movie *True Spirit*, about 16-year-old Jessica Watson's experiences of circumnavigating the world solo for 210 days. There were times when she felt *damned* depressed and lonely out there. So I find it ironic that very shortly after the C-word, Generative AI was on the scene, with many using it to replace human-to-human connections in both verbal (voice and digital avatar tools) and written (content creation tools) forms.

Why are we allowing this to happen? Have we forgotten how we felt when we couldn't be in the presence of real humans?

We can't completely remove humans from client interactions

I've talked a bit about networking and how human connections are vital for our overall sense of security, safety and wellbeing. Let's delve deeper into the importance of human connection from a customer point of view.

As a consumer, I'm guessing you want to feel seen and heard, rather than treated like a number. Yes? Even when we *know* deep down that a business serves multiple people each day, we still want to feel like we matter. We hate being ignored at restaurants where wait staff seem uninterested in taking our orders. We get frustrated when we're left on hold listening to repetitive music for hours. And we get annoyed by retail staff who seem more interested in their own conversations than in offering assistance when we're clearly confused and not just "browsing".

Some places now feature QR codes at tables to place orders, chatbots on their websites, and in-store self-serve kiosks or devices to request information about certain products. These are all great offerings, but what happens when the QR code doesn't work? Or when the chatbot sends you round and round in circles, never answering your question? And when the kiosk is unable to tell you what an eight-year-old boy is likely to like as a birthday gift?

That's when we need the humans to step in. I strongly believe they can never be completely removed. And I've only just touched upon one-off transactions here; what about when you're regularly spending a fair chunk of money on a product or service? You expect consistent, high-quality customer service, right?

When it came to starting a family, my husband and I decided to go down the private hospital route, which meant practically taking out a second mortgage to bring an obstetrician on board. While I was pretty chilled throughout my first pregnancy rather than panic-stricken, I still didn't appreciate how I was treated by our obstetrician. He might have scored top marks in medical school, but he was severely lacking in the customer service department.

For every appointment, we'd always be left waiting for ages in the *crowded* waiting room. It was a long time ago now, but I'm pretty sure the wait time was about 1.5 hours once. And there was never an apology when we were finally called upon. I'd completely understand if the wait was because he was delivering a baby, but I think that was only the case once. Most of the time, he'd just overbooked himself or continually underestimated how much time the typical patient needed or wanted. Anyway, once we were finally in the room, he'd say a brief hello, take a quick look at his notes and say something like, "Ah, you're at Week 28. That means…".

His approach was so generic, and I felt unseen. Not cool at all.

Oh, and to make matters worse, I was regularly told off for gaining too much weight during my pregnancy. Are you kidding me? In my first trimester, the kilos were piling on because I was constantly eating to keep nausea away. I wasn't "blessed" with morning sickness to keep my weight in check. I also didn't appreciate his condescending gold-sticker strategy when I managed to maintain a "good" weight in between check-ups.

So, as soon as I discovered I was pregnant with my second child, I booked an appointment with a different obstetrician – someone a bunch of women in my first-time-mum friendship group raved about. This guy took a completely different approach. My husband and I never waited for more than 10 minutes in the *empty* waiting room. After being welcomed into the consulting room, he'd then lean back in his chair and spend a good ten minutes or so *asking us about our lives* and talking about non-baby stuff. *Then* he'd talk about the pregnancy and do a scan or whatever. Needless to say, I had a *much* better experience with this doctor.

Here we have two obstetricians who had the same role: to nurture and support women bringing new lives into this world. Who do you think I'm more likely to recommend?

Human connection must remain a priority

Bringing AI back into the picture, you must remember this essential tip: please, *do not* overlook the humans for the sake of making more money or increasing productivity. I'm seeing too many business executives and entrepreneurs focus on the wrong things. They're falling into the trap of sourcing and embracing AI tools with the hope of enhancing productivity within the workforce – without considering the impact on the humans on the other side.

This can be seen from two perspectives: the customer experience (external) and the employee experience (internal).

The (external) customer experience

Maybe you're excited about the 20 juicy thought-leadership articles your GenAI just pumped out in the blink of an eye. Or, maybe you've come across this incredible sales bot that can make 1,000 calls while you make a cup of tea. Oh, the productivity!

But have you taken a moment to think about how these processes will be received by your ideal or current clients? Are they likely to connect with the lifeless AI-generated words in your article, or are they more likely to simply skip over it after seeing typical AI words like "unlock" or "unleash" in the heading? And are they going to appreciate some random robot interrupting their day to sell them something they don't think they want or need?

If you answered "no" then I highly recommend you keep reading this book. I have so much to share (and rant about) on the subject. For now, just take this moment to reflect on your current habits, projects and impact.

The (internal) employee experience

Maybe you've decided to introduce agentic AI and have AI bots running workflows and automations. Or, maybe you're asking your tools to create *all* your marketing strategies and write your content.

Have you taken a moment to ask your valuable staff members how they feel about these changes? Are you including them in the process and training them to understand how the new AI tools and processes work – or are you giving them the sack? If it's the latter, you need to be aware of the repercussions of your decisions in the long run. Have you now left an extremely qualified genius with a family to feed jobless? And for what – to rely upon AI bots that are the equivalent of toddlers in intellect and ability and require skilled human management? (I'll talk more about this topic in the next chapter.)

You might have already made some big, messy decisions that have had a negative impact on your staff. Hopefully, it's not too late to turn things around (even if it means kissing the feet of that ex-employee you replaced with AI last month).

My main message here? Ensure you're not getting caught up in the shiny AI vortex and unnecessarily overinvesting in these tools. We must all be more strategic when making AI-related decisions and think about the human impact.

Hear from the humans
Kerryn Powell, The Network Catalyst

I believe human connection isn't a luxury. It's a necessity and core to being human. AI can provide solutions, help problem-solve and get the job done. But without any emotional intelligence (EQ) to draw on, it lacks heart at this point. From decades connecting humans with what they need and facilitating conversations, I've seen how people come alive when they engage with one another – sharing stories that inspire and lessons that guide.

One powerful example comes from a conversation I had with a woman new to networking. Overwhelmed and unsure of where to begin, she came along to my facilitated business networking event. She discovered not just how to connect but how to thrive. Her transformation – from hesitant participant to confident entrepreneur – was sparked by conversations where experiences were exchanged and vulnerabilities shared. She later told me, "I wouldn't still be in business without this".

While AI tools process data, humans process emotions, intuition and context. Our stories create empathy and foster connections that AI simply can't replicate. As I often say, there is no body language on a keyboard. We gain so much when we engage in real-time, authentic connection.

Trust is the foundation of business relationships – and building trust requires intention. It begins with integrity. We need to stand by our values, even in challenging times. I encourage you not to see AI as a shortcut. See it as a way to free up the mental and emotional bandwidth needed to engage meaningfully.

Final thoughts...

In this new world of AI, the value of human connection is becoming increasingly important.

While technology offers us tools to enhance productivity and streamline processes, it's our humanity that truly sets us apart. AI may assist with strategies and communication, but it's the human moments, like the heartfelt conversations, the shared experiences and the personal touches that leave a lasting impression.

AI-generated chapter summary *(with human tweaks)*

- Entrepreneurs often face isolation, making networking and community crucial for support and success.
- Human connection is vital – as humans we are "programmed" to crave belonging and security.
- Stress and anxiety, heightened in modern business contexts, are exacerbated by uncertainties like AI's rapid evolution.
- The COVID-19 pandemic highlighted the profound need for human interaction and the impact of its absence.
- While AI can enhance productivity, it cannot replace emotional support, shared experiences or personal touches.
- Consumers value personalised experiences – they want to "feel seen and heard", not be treated like a number.

- There's an overemphasis on AI, and productivity risks eroding authentic human connection in both internal (employee) and external (customer) interactions.
- Maintaining a human-first approach is essential for both customer satisfaction and team morale.
- Balancing AI's capabilities with intentional human interaction is key to long-term success and meaningful impact.

Chapter 3

Maintaining a "Human-first" Business

"Business should be high tech,
but also high human touch."

Amanda Stevens

AI is undeniably powerful when it comes to processing large amounts of data, generating drafts and analysing trends. It's also incredibly efficient when dealing with repetitive tasks, such as producing outlines or pulling insights from mountains of information. You know, the boring stuff.

Well, it's boring for me. I know plenty of professionals who absolutely love sinking their teeth into spreadsheets, graphs and numbers, then creating big-arse analytical reports, but that's my biggest nightmare. When it comes to actioning that stuff for my business, I'm more than happy to collaborate with AI to get it done – or just hand it all over to a real-life human expert to deal with! On the other hand, there are professionals out there who absolutely despise writing articles and developing marketing strategies – they'd do absolutely anything to avoid it – while content marketers like me don't *want* to hand over our passions to AI. We love doing this stuff ourselves.

If you *really* enjoy doing a particular aspect of your work, please don't feel compelled or pressured to ask AI to do it for the sake of *productivity*. Otherwise, it will feel like you're unwillingly selling your soul to the devil. And you'll be left feeling empty inside.

For me, writing has been my number-one skill since I was a child. I still remember a short story I wrote in Year Two about seeing a white kitten in the pet shop window – I absolutely nailed the spelling, grammar and punctuation (something that many grown-ups still struggle with). For me, the "rules" of writing in the English language have always made sense. And as the years passed, I've become more and more familiar with those rules – and felt more and more entitled to break them.

(You've probably already noticed that I like to start sentences with words like "and", as I just did above. I also love starting with "but" and "because". I enjoy throwing schooling structures like that out the window. *But why, Leanne?* Because I can. Haha!)

You might feel this comfort and familiarity with mathematical equations. Scientific calculations. Strategies. Analytics. Reporting. Event planning. Managing or motivating people. Sales. Social media. Whatever it is, if you've got a natural talent or developed a real skill for something, I strongly encourage holding onto that – no matter what the future holds for AI.

Saying that, we can't completely bury our heads in the sand and pretend AI isn't here. We also don't want to be overtaken by our competitors who *are* embracing it. So, we need to find ways to use AI to make tweaks or amplify our human experience and expertise. We just need to understand how to do it effectively, efficiently and safely.

Handle the "AI-first" craze with care

Apparently, there's a sense of urgency for many organisations out there to be known as "AI-first". I'm seeing AI trainers across the globe promoting it and massive companies proudly announcing as a badge of honour that they've embraced the concept. But I'm a bit wary about it.

Let's start by breaking down the definition. "AI-first" refers to a strategy or approach where AI is at the core of an organisation's operations, decision-making and customer experience. To put it simply, it means being hyper-focused on the possibilities for inserting AI into every nook and cranny possible to enhance productivity.

That's all well and good, but I believe if your organisation wants to go down the "AI-first" path, extra emphasis needs to go into supporting your staff via human connection – especially when the whole concept of humans being replaced by AI has resulted in insomnia for hundreds of thousands across the globe.

While us non-techy folk are new to this term, it's actually been around for a little while. Salesforce CEO and Co-founder Marc Benioff made the declaration that "Salesforce will become an AI-first company" at an internal company-wide meeting back in 2014. Since then, the cloud-based customer relationship management (CRM) platform has continually been upgraded with technology to manage and further improve customer interactions across sales, service, marketing and commerce. More recently, they've been putting a lot of focus on building 'Agentforce', which uses AI to create autonomous agents (aka AI staff) to assist their clients' employees and customers. (We'll talk more about AI agents in Chapter 10: Bots in the Back Office.)

In a January 2025 interview with Harry Stebbings, Benioff talked about Agentforce with great enthusiasm, saying he's moved his "whole support infrastructure to the agentic platform" and will move his whole sales platform to the agentic platform as well, "for no other reason but to show my customers what is possible. I think we are in such a new world right now in terms of what is possible today, versus even just six months ago, that customers do not understand what it could mean for them".

Benioff says he's likely to continue pushing Agentforce and "rebalancing" his workforce by moving people out of support roles and into sales or other opportunities within the company. The fact that human staff aren't just being sacked due to AI developments is music to my ears. However, I do hope the whole change management process is tackled with sensitivity, keeping human emotions and mental load in check throughout the potentially massive shifts ahead.

IBM is another large, well-known organisation proudly embracing the AI-first approach. In October 2024, IBM CEO Arvind Krishna said businesses that build their operations around AI will ultimately lead in productivity and growth.

While this is true, I'm seeing so many examples of humans being forgotten in the process. I know of at least two marketing agencies that have sacked their whole copywriting teams following the release of ChatGPT. These kneejerk reactions are often the result of messaging from the big players like Salesforce and IBM, as well as the media.

When I hear "AI-first", I get an image of someone throwing all their eggs into a basket labelled "Artificial Intelligence", which is a strategy that could have negative repercussions on human employees and humanity as a whole if we're not careful. Hopefully, the work cultures at Salesforce and IBM support healthy, thriving humans who live with purpose and without constantly being in fear of being replaced by AI in the near future.

Ensuring a "human-first" business

When it comes to AI, shiny object syndrome comes into play. Yes, it can be extremely useful at times. Yes, it can increase productivity because it can do things way quicker (and sometimes better) than humans. And, yes, it can handle loads of data in seconds that a human would otherwise require days or weeks to process. I get all that. AI has its place.

But we can't hand over *everything* to the bots. We need to consider carefully where to draw the line. When is it okay to ask an AI agent to take complete control over a task, and when is it just laziness? Just imagine if we *did* hand over full control to AI and the bots ruled the world. Human society as we know it would implode.

I much prefer the idea of being "human-first" with AI usage. It's fine for AI to come out to play, but we need humans to tell it when to go away. (Sounds like a fun, modern nursery rhyme, doesn't it?) I crave human connection, as do most of us in some shape or form. I remain determined to find ways to use AI to empower people, boost creativity and drive ethical, transparent practices. These beliefs and values sit at the very core of this book, and are supported by research conducted by Dr Renée Richardson Gosline and Yunhao Zhang, which we'll assess shortly.

To me, a "human-first" approach involves *using AI thoughtfully to amplify human skills and maintain what makes us unique.* Humans should remain the primary, not secondary, focus within an organisation.

This means rather than sacking human employees and replacing them with bots that can do things faster and apparently better, we need to be investing in the humans instead – offering training so they understand how to use various AI tools to complement their expertise and experience. We should empower them and make them feel like they still have a place in the workforce. No one should be left feeling redundant or vulnerable right now. Everyone should feel safe and made aware of opportunities to shift focus and pivot into different roles within the company if need be.

Most importantly, when it comes to AI, you *always* need expert humans to keep an eye on the bots and output produced. You also need humans to be prepared to make tweaks and mention concerns or issues to their managers. And you need them to handle tasks manually if the technology fails for one reason or another.

If you sack all the humans because someone has "figured out" a way for technology to take the place of their pay cheque, you're opening yourself up to extensive trouble down the track. Introduce AI tools and agents to your organisation, no worries. It's the future. You'll be left behind if you don't at least consider different tools and processes. Yada, yada, yada. Just ensure there are always humans – or at least one experienced human – ready to challenge the bots with their human-centred opinions.

A human-first approach also involves keeping humans at the heart of customer interactions, ensuring experiences feel personal and authentic.

So, I beg you not to jump onboard the digital avatar bandwagon thinking all those AI-generated videos will actually connect with your viewers. And don't replace all customer interactions with AI phone agents and chatbots without any clear processes and opportunities for real-life human employees to come onboard. And don't use AI to pump out all your marketing content without anyone available to double-check brand voice and messaging.

There are "correct" ways to address these processes, which I'll cover later in the book. The short tip for now is, whatever you do, don't fall into the trap of being hyper-focused on productivity and forgetting about the impact on the clients on the other side. If you lose their trust through AI misuse or abuse, it will be extremely hard to build it back up.

Ultimately humans favour humans

Dr Renée Richardson Gosline is an Senior Lecturer & Research Scientist at Massachusetts Institute of Technology (MIT) and is head of the Human-First AI group at MIT's Initiative on The Digital Economy. She's completely onboard with the human-first AI approach, believing that AI should serve as a collaborator, not a replacement, in human-led processes.

Along with Yunhao Zhang, Dr Gosline has led extensive research and oversight of programs at MIT to lead the way for human-first AI collaboration. This includes a 2023 study that tested four avenues of content creation: AI only, human only, human with AI references and AI with human references. It found that while most of the 1212 participants agreed on the high quality of AI-generated content: "Participants felt more satisfied with the content and were willing to pay more if they were informed that the content was created solely by a human expert." Basically, they felt there was a higher emotional and actual value attached due to the perception of quality.

This fills me with so much hope. Because while we all know AI *can* generate amazing stuff, the research shows that humans still prefer humans. There's something to keep in mind next time your tired brain feels compelled to pump out an article, email or LinkedIn post from your GenAI without a second thought. It also indicates a real need to educate your employees on how AI works to ensure their usage remains as ethical, fair and aligned with human values as possible. If we're using AI for productivity purposes, we don't want it to be at the detriment of the client relationship. The humans need to still shine through.

I believe building trust through transparency will be absolutely vital as technology advances. Businesses will need to be upfront about when and how AI is used – whether in customer service, content creation or decision-making. Hidden automation can otherwise lead to scepticism. However, we need to tread lightly, because, as highlighted in the study, "revealing the source of content production reduces – but does not reverse – the perceived quality gap between human and AI-generated content". In other words, if your customers get even a whiff of AI content or processes from your organisation, it's likely to make them somewhat wary. It makes sense, though – soon it will become harder and harder to determine where the humans end and the AI begins, and nobody wants to feel misinformed or misdirected. I predict this sense of uncertainty will continue for a few more years, especially around those who abuse AI for deep fakes and scams.

Even though there's the potential to reduce human labour, the research warns that the "results by no means suggest that LLMs should completely replace human agents – especially human oversight". Yes! I totally agree. Especially because this oversight is still required to ensure GenAI output handles sensitive topics adequately and inappropriate information is never distributed. Imagine the hot water you could find yourself in if you didn't double-check something like that. We simply can't be handing over full control to the bots. AI output can never be perceived as one-size-fits-all. We also have no idea of the methods and resources involved in the pre-training steps behind the scenes either.

To summarise the research: we must ensure our clients are front of mind as soon as AI enters the equation. Trust can easily erode and is hard (or impossible) to rebuild. So, it's vital to keep the humans happy to keep your business bank account happy!

Hear from the humans
Amanda Stevens, consumer futurist

We are heading into an era where brand trust is formed very differently from five years ago. Distrust is building and people are developing a lens for detecting AI-generated content. When I read something online, I often think, *Did AI write this?* If it feels robotic or impersonal, I move on. This is a major challenge for brands. They risk losing trust if they don't maintain transparency and authenticity.

AI needs to be trained on your brand's voice and values. It should enhance human relationships rather than replace them. For instance, customer-service bots can handle low-level tasks but must always offer an option to speak to a human. The human connection is irreplaceable.

Brand trust takes years to build but can be lost in a second – whether it's due to data breaches or misuse of AI, like obvious generative content that erodes the "know, like, trust" factor. Missteps, like overusing bots or creating generic outputs, could lead to significant trust erosion.

The balance lies in keeping AI as a tool for efficiency while always adding a human layer. The customer experience must remain emotionally engaging and relational rather than transactional. Business should be high-tech, but also high human touch.

Balancing the AI tools with our human brains

As mentioned earlier, AI can be extremely helpful. And it's likely to be heavily embedded into our futures, so it can't be ignored. However, I want you to be wary of the times when it feels so much *easier* to just ask AI to do stuff for you – like when you're feeling exhausted, overwhelmed or (ahem) lazy. It's the laziness factor we need to be particularly aware of.

If you're feeling worn out, please go take a nap, meditate or grab some fresh air. It will have a much more positive impact on you in the long term. Because if you make a habit of relying on AI to do all your thinking for you, you put yourself at risk of understimulating your brain and winding up with the equivalent of mashed potato in your head. Mindless social media doomscrolling and stupid YouTube videos have already caused enough damage to us all. As I mentioned in Chapter 1: Let's Press Pause, you want to ensure that AI is fuelling your creativity – not replacing it completely.

If your company is not strategic with how it incorporates AI, it opens itself up to massive risk. Customers will just see right through obvious AI-generated information and interactions, leading to diminished reputation or loss of business. But if you ensure the humans are always in control, you're in a much safer position. We'll talk more about the ethics, intellectual property (IP) and cybersecurity later in the book.

Minding our manners

I want to throw in an interesting titbit here about one way I aim to "keep it human" when using AI: saying "please" and "thank you" in my prompts. (I talk more about this in Chapter 4: Prompt Engineering 101, but basically, prompts are instructions or briefings you provide to AI tools.) While I joke when I say that I maintain politeness because I want the robots to remember I'm "one of the nice ones" when they take over one day, there is some truth to it. The LLMs are learning from us right now, so we have this responsibility as their human drivers to teach them right from wrong. We're also more likely to see higher quality output when we treat them with respect.

According to Dr Eduardo Benitez Sandoval, Social Robotics Researcher at the University of New South Wales School of Art & Design, politeness has practical effects in helping humans avoid conflicts, promoting diplomacy and allowing cultural exchange. Since AI tools are trained on human behaviour, it makes sense for us to treat them the same way:

> *Politeness might be advantageous for us as users because it somewhat encourages clarity and, therefore, efficiency, which is what we expect when interacting with machines. When we're polite ... we might receive more detailed, understandable or helpful responses from our AI.*

I totally agree with that last part. I don't know about you, but I was taught the importance of manners from a very young age. While it sounds silly, I even told my babies to say "ta" at the end of a breastfeed – despite them being many months away from actually saying it. My fear is that if we start forgetting to say "please" and "thank you" to our AI tools, these poor habits will flow into our real-life human interactions as well. Especially now that voice prompting is becoming more readily available – it will be all too easy to shout demands at your AI robot, then turn to the person beside you and continue with that rude tone when you speak to them.

This scenario is comparable to a story from my university days, back when SMS shorthand was becoming a thing. Despite finishing Unit 4 English at high school (and getting 48 out of 50 for my final-assessment short story, thank-you-very-much), I had fallen into the habit of texting things like "coz" and "cu l8er" when messaging mates. At first, I didn't see the harm in it because everyone else was doing the same thing. But then one day I was checking one of my university essays before submission and was horrified to see that some of this shorthand had snuck its way in. #howembarrassing.

From that day forward, I decided to always write out my messages in full – even though it makes me sound like an old woman. My aim was to streamline my writing across *all* channels so I wouldn't fall into that trap again.

I feel the same about how I speak to my AI tools. I'm respectful. I offer corrections in a kind way – unless it really, *really* doesn't get it. (But my frustrations with a bot probably say more about my stress levels at the time, rather than the bot itself!) Whatever instructions I pop in or responses I get back, I'm always conscious about saying "please" and "thank you". It's simply the right thing to do – and it's what I would do if I were interacting with a human assistant. So, it's a healthy habit to get into and maintain.

I'm not the only one who uses manners with my AI tools. Many people I've spoken to throughout my AI journey admit to doing the same thing. Others don't agree. I once commented on a LinkedIn post of an AI enthusiast who had provided some prompt ideas to her audience – they sounded like demands, without any semblance of manners. I said that while I liked the prompts, I would personally also add "please" and "thank you". Her reply? "Umm, but why? You wouldn't say thank you to your toaster, would you?" I came back with some smartarse comment like "Sometimes I do!" But I think she missed the point. A toaster isn't constantly learning from how we interact with it (at least for now). LLMs *are* learning from us. We have the responsibility to show respect and build tools that are respectful back to us. We need to speak to them the same way we speak to colleagues, employees, friends and family members.

Final thoughts...

It's important to remember that the tools are still learning – from us. Yes, they're going to get stuff wrong from time to time. But you need to be the bigger (and only) person in the situation. Accept there are times when you just have to use your human brain or ask a fellow expert human to get the job done right.

If you're part of a massive organisation, you probably have IT teams managing the big data AI projects. I hope there are plenty of human experts driving those projects and ensuring humans aren't forgotten in the process. If you're self-employed or running a small team, I hope you're not getting caught up in the AI hype and thinking it's going to solve all your issues. It can help, sure, but communication among human staff or getting the right staff onboard will serve you better.

I urge you to fight for a human-first business – a business where the humans are managing, rather than being replaced by the AI tools, left, right and centre. Why would we want that? Remember what I said in the previous chapter about human connection? That's what we truly want. Personally, I love how AI supports me with projects when I have a limited supply of time or headspace. And I love watching the a-ha moments when my students learn how to use AI as a knowledgeable sidekick, rather than allowing it to take over as the poorly trained hero of their story.

You have a choice right now: will you let AI amplify your team's human skills or allow it to take them away?

AI-generated chapter summary *(with human tweaks)*

- AI-first is an approach where AI is at the centre of business operations, decision-making and customer interactions.

- Companies like Salesforce and IBM have embraced AI-first strategies, integrating AI-driven automation, predictive analytics and autonomous agents.

- While AI-first businesses can boost efficiency, they risk sidelining human expertise, leading to impersonal interactions and workforce displacement.

- Human-first businesses use AI to support, rather than replace, human skills – ensuring technology enhances creativity, problem-solving and personalisation.

- Maintaining human oversight in AI processes prevents errors, biases and trust issues that arise from unchecked automation.

- Research shows people still prefer human-created content over AI-generated material, highlighting the importance of authenticity in branding and communication.

- Over-reliance on AI can erode customer trust, especially when businesses fail to disclose AI involvement in content creation and service interactions.

- Using AI with intentionality, rather than as a shortcut, ensures businesses stay ethical, competitive and human-centric in an increasingly digital world.

PART II

ARTIFICIAL
INTELLIGENCE

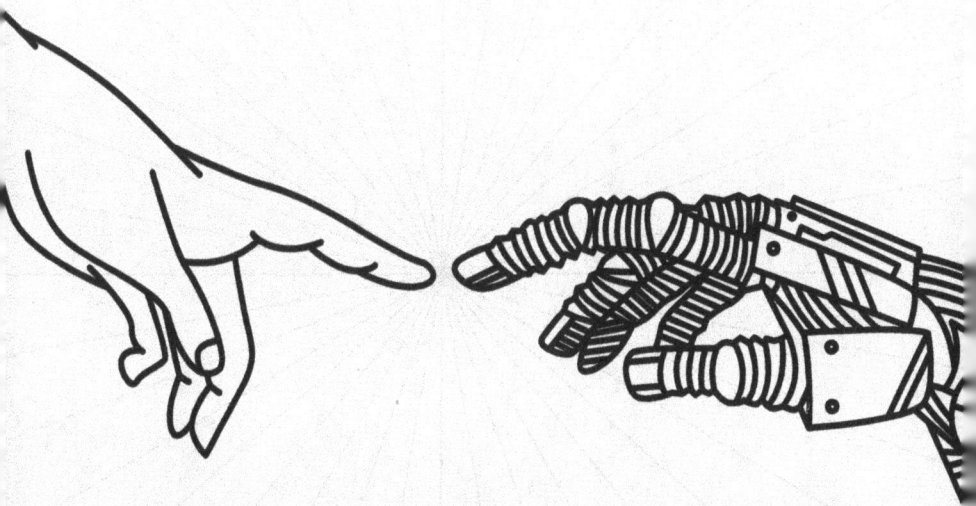

PART II

ARTIFICIAL
INTELLIGENCE

Chapter 4

Prompt Engineering 101

*"Prompting is not a technical skill. It's first and foremost
a communication skill. AI has immense knowledge –
but it lacks human wisdom and curiosity, so it needs
clear intent and guidance."*

Adam Walsh

I still remember the very first time I logged into ChatGPT in early
2023. While I was extremely inexperienced in AI, I was a very
experienced human copywriter with a content marketing agency
that was starting to struggle. I was curious about this shiny new
(and free) threat that had crash-landed into my arena. How dare
it! I remember my eyes scanning the basic page before me, then
landing on the message bar, which looked very similar to the
Google search bar I'd grown to know and trust. It was then that
I plugged in my first ever prompt:

Why are copywriters better than ChatGPT?

Okay, yes, I was curious and just a *little* bit bitter – like all the other
copywriters who were slowly creeping out of denial and starting to
see the writing on the wall. However, I admit to instantly feeling a
glimmer of hope when I witnessed extremely generic and robotic

words fill my screen. "Oh, this is crap!" I exclaimed out loud. "I could write sooo much better than this!"

Initially, I thought that was all I was up against. I hadn't discovered prompt engineering yet. And I had no idea what greatness could be achieved after training up the tool. As a self-proclaimed non-techy professional woman, I hadn't yet realised that I had the ability to turn ChatGPT into a highly valued member of my team.

Fast-forward a few months and I was starting to get it. I'd read *The Art of Prompt Engineering with ChatGPT* by Nathan Hunter, which explained everything in an easy-to-understand way. I had listened to a few podcasts. And I'd followed some AI enthusiasts on LinkedIn. As mentioned in the prologue, I then threw together a free webinar on "How to use ChatGPT and still sound human", helping to cement my new-found knowledge by teaching others. And I've been teaching this topic ever since, even calling myself a "prompt engineer" from time to time.

More than two years later, I'm still meeting professionals who have no idea what prompt engineering is. Maybe that's you? Well, while the words "prompt engineering" can send non-techy people into a sweaty panic, it's actually not as bad as you think. You don't need to be an IT geek or guru to get it. You don't need to understand coding. And you don't need to remember any specific formulas (and thank f*ck for that, because I would struggle massively if that were the case!). To put it simply, prompt engineering is all about crafting and tweaking instructions provided to a GenAI tool to ensure it delivers accurate and effective results.

Yep, that's it.

Now we're getting into the juicy prompt engineering stuff – the stuff you've been itching to sink your claws into since Chapter 1. If you've skipped ahead to this page, please head back to Part I – Humans, you cheeky monkey. Getting into the right mindset is essential before diving into this section. Trust me. It will set you apart from, like, 90% of the population.*

In this chapter, my aim is to flip your thinking on what the precious words "prompt engineering" mean in the AI world. And I'll explain how it all works. I think you'll be pleasantly surprised. Some of these upcoming gold nuggets have been complete game-changers for the majority of my students and audiences.

What is prompt engineering?

It it absolutely key to provide GenAI tools with clear written or verbal instructions – otherwise known as "prompts". When you don't provide enough clarity or context, you're looking at a pure example of "garbage in, garbage out". Insert crappy, basic instructions and you can expect crappy, basic results. (The human copywriter within me screams every time I see this type of content published.)

From my experience, the majority of people are treating the GenAI message bar the same way they use the Google search bar. You know, smashing out demands for quick results:

Write me this!
What's the answer for that?
Give me this!
Can you fix that?

You may be guilty of this too. But I'm here to tell you that while they look similar, these bars are *not* the same thing. With GenAI, you can't just throw in a basic command and expect gold on the first go. It's just not going to happen. When it comes to best prompt practices, it's not about *what* you ask AI to do but *how* you ask it.

If your prompt doesn't clearly outline exactly what you need, you're going to struggle to get effective results. And that quite

---

* Completely made up – but likely correct – statistic by me.

often means wasting time, going backwards and forwards in an argument with your bot when you could have simply written or researched the information yourself! However, unlike maths equations, there are no *exact* prompts that you *must* use to ensure high quality. Honestly, I could plug in one prompt one day and get a certain response, and the very next day I could try it again and get something completely different.

What do you mean, Leanne? I have to come up with the prompts myself? But I have no idea what I'm doing with AI!

If that sounds like you, you're not alone. Discovering and uncovering the perfect prompts has been a barrier to entry for so many professionals and entrepreneurs. But trust me, there's no need to waste energy trying to source the perfect prompt for your needs. As mentioned in Chapter 1: Let's Press Pause, I purchased one of those "1,000 prompts for $57" deals back when I started my AI journey and, honestly, I think I've only ever looked at it once, maybe twice. Whenever you come across generic prompts shared by AI enthusiasts and experts, they need to be seen as excellent starting points – nothing more.

Do you want to know why? Because those humans don't know you. They don't know your role, your company and your clients. They don't know what projects you've got coming up and what your priorities are. (Unless, of course, you've developed a strong human connection with them, as outlined in Chapter 2: The Importance of Human Connection!) Sure, they're keen to help you, and that's why they're sharing the information. But there's usually an agenda. They're trying to build your trust and pull you towards their pricey programs and podcasts. I get it – that's the whole point of content creation, after all. However, many of these prompts are also 100% AI-generated, and in many cases they haven't been tested to check the quality of output.

When I run AI workshops and programs, I'm always transparent with my clients when I ask tools to supply sample prompts for their

Prompt eGuides. Because unless they're in marketing, in many cases I wouldn't have the fuzziest idea what they do in their day-to-day roles and what wording would go into a decent prompt. But that's when we kick off the fun collaboration and critical thinking process. I get them to suggest and decide what should be changed and added. You ultimately need to make *all* prompts your own, because *you* are the human expert here.

Are there any 'magic' AI formulas?

As a content marketer and strategist, I admit to never following any prompt formulas or templates. I just think about the desired output (aka result) and work backwards from there, thinking about all the elements that must be included in the plan or content. But if you're an absolute AI newbie, you might find comfort in ticking off a checklist. Then you know you're entering all the essential information into the GenAI message bar without missing anything.

If that's the case, you can start with a formula until you become more comfortable with the prompting process. (I have another trick up my sleeve that will help, but I'll talk about that shortly.) I've pulled together a basic prompting formula for you as a starting point. I recommend including as many of these elements as possible into your initial prompt, as it will save you hours in the long run. If you forget an element, no worries – you can always "re-brief" the AI tool later.

Here are the core elements to be featured in a high-quality prompt:

- **Task.** You want to kick things off with a clear action and specific goal. This one should be fairly obvious.

  Example: "Please create a list of 5 × social media posts, approximately 150–200 words each, to promote an AI training program targeting business executives."

- **Context.** Provide background information to improve the response, including purpose, audience and platform. You'd typically find this information in a human-to-human project briefing.

  Example: "The training program is aimed at business executives who want to stay ahead of the curve by integrating AI into their leadership and decision-making. The focus is on positioning AI as a tool for smarter, faster decisions and streamlining operations. We'll be focusing on the LinkedIn platform, with the goal of driving registrations and building thought leadership around AI training."

- **Sample content.** To steer AI in the right direction, it's a good idea to include examples of what a "good" output looks like. You can provide past examples written by your team or something you've discovered externally for "inspiration". (I'm not going to promote plagiarism here!)

  Example: "Please use a style similar to these:
  - Feeling swamped by AI hype? Discover how to cut through the noise and use AI to make smarter business decisions.
  - AI isn't just for techies – it's for leaders like you. Learn how to guide your team into the future with confidence in our upcoming AI training."

- **Persona.** You don't always have to do this, but I've found telling the AI who it's supposed to "be" while working on the task often improves the quality of the response.

  Example: "Pretend you're a savvy social media marketer who knows how to connect with busy professionals, using a mix of wit, warmth and expertise to engage."

- **Format.** Consider what your ideal output/results will look like. Without clear instructions about the structure and format, your tool will just do whatever it "feels" like!

Example: "Please deliver the posts in full draft form, ready for review. Each post should be 2–3 sentences long and include:

- a compelling hook or question to grab attention
- clear messaging that highlights the benefits of the AI training program for business executives
- a strong call to action (e.g. "Sign up now", or "Learn more").
- relevant hashtags (e.g. #FutureReadyLeadership; #AIForBusiness)
- sparing use of emojis to add visual interest and energy."

- **Tone.** I talk about the importance of tone and brand voice in Chapter 6: Nailing Your Brand Voice. You mightn't need to feature this aspect in every prompt if you've already trained your AI tool to recognise your writing style. (I can't wait to share this stuff with you!) For now, let's just say you may wish to specify the tone within your prompt to ensure it aligns with the vibe you're going for.

Example: "As per the HumanEdge AI Training brand voice, please keep it friendly, relatable and a little cheeky – something that sparks curiosity and makes the audience feel seen."

Add each of those core elements together and you have a fully engineered prompt!

Yes, you'll notice it's long – probably a lot longer than anything you've entered into GenAI to date! But can you see how thorough it is? By including all these details, you have a much greater chance of quality output. With regular use, you can train the tool to get to know you and your business inside and out. These days, I only need to make minor tweaks when I use AI. And it's almost undetectable that I've used my little sidekick!

Let's look at the unedited social media posts my tool produced from the above prompt.

Post one – Cut Through the AI Noise:

💡 *Feeling overwhelmed by all the AI buzzwords and jargon? You're not alone. AI can feel like an intimidating beast, but here's the truth: it's a tool—and a powerful one at that—for leaders like YOU.*

Our AI training program isn't about teaching you to be a programmer. It's about helping you make smarter, faster decisions, streamlining operations, and staying ahead of the game. We'll show you how to take the practical, human-first approach to AI integration in your leadership.

Ready to lead with clarity and confidence in the AI era? Let us guide you. 🚀

☞ *Sign up now: [Insert link]*

#FutureReadyLeadership #AIForBusiness

Post two – Leadership in the AI Era:

AI isn't just for the techies anymore—it's for forward-thinking leaders like you. ✳

The future of leadership demands the ability to combine human insight with AI-powered tools. Our AI training program is designed to give business executives like you the skills to:

✓ *Streamline decision-making processes*
✓ *Identify AI opportunities in your operations*
✓ *Empower your team with future-ready strategies*

We keep things simple, actionable, and tailored for busy leaders. No tech jargon—just practical tools and insights to elevate your leadership game.

💼 *The future is here. Are you ready to embrace it?*

☞ *Learn more and reserve your spot: [Insert link]*

#InnovationLeadership #AIForExecutives

Not too bad. I think it's about 80% to 90% there – and very aligned with my brand. But there's a good reason for that: as mentioned above, my GenAI tool knows me really well now. And it all started with a *proper* AI onboarding process.

What's an AI onboarding process, Leanne? Oh, I'm glad you asked. I'll introduce you to the concept now.

Meet your junior assistant or intern

Okay, get ready to have your mind blown.

When it comes to GenAI or LLM tools like ChatGPT, Copilot and Gemini, please don't approach them like on-demand search engines. Yes, technically that's what they are, but it's time to flick the switch on your thinking. I want you to interact with AI as though it's a *human* junior assistant or intern. Yep, treat it like a human.

Why? Because if you were meeting your human junior assistant on their very first day at the office, would you immediately start shouting vague demands like "Create a business plan for me", or "Write this article", or "Develop a marketing campaign"? Nope. But what if you did? In an attempt to please you, their boss, they'd try to complete the task to the best of their ability. After all, they know how to use the internet, so how hard could it be? The thing is, your junior assistant, on their *very* first day at work, knows *nothing* about your business or customers. So, they're likely to bring back useless results, like:

- a basic business plan that doesn't speak to your industry, your needs or your financial goals
- an article that's bland, lifeless and generic
- a mediocre marketing campaign without an understanding of who it's marketing to and why.

This is exactly what AI is currently producing for hundreds of thousands of people across the globe. And they have no idea why the output is so crappy. As soon as you see AI as a human junior assistant, it changes your thinking. What would you *actually* do on their first day of work? You'd kick things off with an *onboarding process*, right? So that's what you need to do with AI as well. Because to create authentic, high-quality, human-centric content you need to train your AI assistant first to understand your business, your brand voice and, most importantly, your customers.

That's step one, before you do anything else. But it's a step that the majority of the population completely skips over. It's not their fault, though – they don't know what they don't know. But now you *do* know. And we're going to work through the business onboarding process together in the following chapters. Once you complete that valuable initial step, you can start producing real magic – and bring on AI as a valuable extension of your team. Without replacing you, the human, of course!

Final thoughts...

I hope you're feeling a little less intimidated about prompts now. Because prompt engineering isn't rocket science (even though many AI enthusiasts online seem to completely overcomplicate things). It's just a matter of crafting clear, purposeful instructions and letting your expertise shine through. If you treat AI like your eager (but clueless) junior assistant, you'll begin to see phenomenal results.

AI-generated chapter summary *(with human tweaks)*

- "Garbage in, garbage out." The quality of AI output depends entirely on the clarity and specificity of the input prompt.

- Generative AI tools like ChatGPT are not Google search bars. They require carefully crafted instructions to deliver valuable results.

- Prompt engineering is about crafting and refining instructions to guide AI effectively.

- Generic pre-made prompts are only starting points. They must be personalised to align with your role, business, and audience needs.

- Core elements of a high-quality prompt include:
  - *Task.* Clearly define the action and goal.
  - *Context.* Share relevant background and audience details.
  - *Sample content.* Offer examples of the style or output you want.
  - *Persona.* Specify the role or tone AI should adopt.
  - *Format.* Indicate the structure or style required.
  - *Tone.* Match the desired voice, such as friendly, cheeky or professional.

- A detailed prompt ensures the output is more aligned with your needs, saving time and reducing frustration.

- Treat AI like a junior assistant who requires onboarding to learn about your business, brand voice and audience before expecting quality results.

Chapter 5

Briefing the Bot About Your Business

"AI can't read our minds – just like humans can't.
It requires clear instructions, context, and access to the
right tools to get the job done effectively."

Dan Sanchez

When China launched DeepSeek in early 2025, the world had a collective meltdown – some buzzing with excitement, others breaking into a cold sweat over the billions sunk into competing AI tools. As someone who's never in my life even considered lining up for hours to be among the first to purchase anything, I just sat back and watched while other AI enthusiasts quickly jumped onto the "new tool" bandwagon. They were swiftly producing videos and graphics to show off prompts and tactics for handling DeepSeek, and raving about the quality of output and comparing it to its counterparts.

But I noticed that everything they showed was missing one vital component: true personalisation to one's business. No one was talking about it. Maybe because the security and privacy aspects had yet to be explored. Or, maybe because they were unaware of the power of the onboarding process for high-quality, human-centric results.

I personally had no desire to jump onboard and start using a new tool when my ChatGPT junior assistant knows me so well. It meets my requirements perfectly well, so I didn't see the need to complicate things by getting involved with experimentation. And I definitely didn't need to be caught up in shiny things at the time, because I had a manuscript deadline looming!

As I've already mentioned, it's very easy to get caught up in the AI hype. But we need to bring it all back to one core question: *If AI is meant to enhance my productivity, is it productive to endlessly research and experiment with new AI tools instead of actually doing the day-to-day work I'm actually paid to do?* While it might seem easier (and possibly more fun) to spend time chasing technological advancements, you're much better off investing your time into training ChatGPT, Copilot or Gemini to truly understand your business. If you go back to the absolute basics right now, you'll see higher quality results in the future. New shiny updates will keep on coming, but they mean absolutely nothing if you haven't trained your AI to serve you effectively.

In this chapter, we'll kick off the onboarding (aka training) process with your "junior assistant". You can't skip this step if you want to ensure quality results from your AI tool of choice – for both internal and external purposes. In the future, AI tools may prompt you directly to assist with their own training. I look forward to seeing that! But, right now, you need to take the lead. Understanding how to train your AI properly ensures that you remain in control, rather than becoming a slave to the tech, blindly trusting whatever output it generates.

Why does AI need to know about our business?

Artificial intelligence can only achieve so much on its own. It's been pre-trained with loads and loads of data and information that some engineers decided was relevant. We have no idea where it was all sourced from and whether it was even sourced ethically with permission from the original sources. That includes articles allegedly used to train and inform the AI without consent or payment, which a range of publishers are currently (as of February 2025) making legal claims against for major copyright infringement. I don't blame them for being annoyed; I would be too!

Ethical implications aside, the most important factor to consider is that if we only pull information from what the tool has been pre-trained with, we'll end up with generic, uncustomised results. If we don't teach the tool properly about the context it's working within, we're never going to get quality results. In a professional context, this is absolutely vital. You need to train the tool to understand what your business offers and what you stand for if you want to develop high-quality, AI-generated systems, processes, strategies and content.

As mentioned in the previous chapter, many people just jump onto their GenAI or LLM and start shouting demands without undergoing any type of onboarding process. So, it makes complete sense why they then bad-mouth AI tools for delivering crappy output that requires so much time to correct. Or it makes sense why your potential clients are bad-mouthing your email, article and social media content, because it sounds as generic as your local supermarket-branded toothpaste.

In the following chapters you'll learn how to start developing completely customised systems, processes, strategies and content. I'm so excited for your journey ahead!

Hear from the humans
Dan Sanchez, Senior AI Marketing Strategist at Social Media Examiner

As AI becomes more integrated into our work, we need to treat it much like we treat our human coworkers. Just as we delegate tasks to people with clear objectives, resources and expectations, we must do the same with AI. And, as AI becomes more capable, the way we delegate will become even more important. That's why, even when writing a prompt, you should think of AI as filling a role. Give it a job description. Provide it with company context, market dynamics and customer insights to help it deliver meaningful results – not just for tasks but for entire projects.

In the future, working with AI will feel a lot like working with humans. In some ways, it will be easier because AI doesn't have morale issues or personal conflicts. But, in other ways, it will be harder, because without the right guardrails AI can quickly veer off track. Setting clear parameters will be crucial.

One thing is certain: AI is joining the workforce. And just like any other tool or team member, the way we guide it will determine its impact.

Time to source those style guides...

To get started, I recommend pulling out your company's brand and communication style guides. You know, the ones collecting proverbial dust in cloud storage. It's probably been a while since you looked at them (or maybe never...?). We're going to start plugging those details into your AI tool.

But I don't have a style guide, Leanne! If that's the case, no worries. I give you permission to jump ahead to the next section of this chapter.

For everyone else, I'm assuming none of the information within your style guides is overly sensitive, and you or your marketing team would be happy to hand it over to a client if requested. (Not that the client would particularly care, but it's a good way to consider things!) You always need to keep this back of mind, especially during the onboarding process.

Ultimately, to train your AI about your business and brand voice you need to enter fairly basic stuff here, like top-level details about your products, services, mission, vision, values and unique selling proposition (USP). There's no need to go into specifics about the costs and profit margins. If you've got the business story or catalyst on file, that might work to add to the mix as well. (This is probably featured somewhere on your "About" page on your website, so this is fine to insert as well.)

Do you have all that information handy? Great! Now it's time to head over to your AI (e.g. ChatGPT, Copilot, Gemini) and insert the following prompt into the general message bar:

Hello. Today, I'd like to train you to gain an understanding about my company, <insert your business name here>, including our products, services, mission, vision and values.

Here's some key information about the company for you to review and refer to: <insert information from your brand/ communication style guide here>. No need to take any further action at this point. Please just review and provide a summary about the company to confirm you understand everything.

Before clicking 'Enter', you can either select the paperclip icon next to the message bar and attach the style guide or copy and paste all the collated information within the <insert information from your brand/communication style guide here> section. It can be long and messy; that's totally fine. The AI will read the information perfectly.

The output (aka response) provided should basically be a repeat of everything you just inserted.

Some tools, like ChatGPT, offer 'memory' features – meaning you can say something like, "Thank you. Please remember this information about <insert your business name here> for future projects".

However, some free tools don't retain memory beyond a single conversation. Always keep a backup of your training prompts in a document so you can quickly retrain AI when needed. And remember never to share confidential or sensitive business data.

No style guide?

All good! The following prompts are for you. But even if you *do* have a style guide, I think you'll still get a lot of value from this section.

If you work for yourself and never got around to establishing a communications and/or brand style guide of your own, or if your company is currently going through a rebrand, your prompt could be more like this:

Hello. Today, I'd like to train you to gain an understanding about my company, <insert your business name>, including our products, services, mission, vision and values. What type of information do you need from me?

Asking the tool for information is an action so many people are completely unaware about, but it can be extremely powerful. It's perfect for when you're struggling to get started and have no idea which resources you should supply to the tool for optimal results.

As an example, I plugged this prompt into Copilot to give you an idea of the type of response you can expect:

Hi there! That sounds like an exciting task. To get a thorough understanding of HumanEdge AI Training, it would be helpful to gather the following information:

1. *Company Overview: A brief description of your company, including its history and founding.*
2. *Mission Statement: What drives your company? What are your core objectives and goals?*
3. *Vision Statement: Where do you see your company heading in the future?*

4. *Core Values: The fundamental beliefs and guiding principles of your company.*

5. *Products and Services: Detailed information about the products and services you offer.*

6. *Target Audience: Who are your main customers or clients?*

7. *Competitive Advantage: What sets your company apart from competitors?*

8. *Success Stories: Any case studies or success stories that highlight your company's impact.*

Let's start with these categories, and if there's more, we can dive in deeper. What would you like to share first?

The AI has now provided questions to spark my thinking. I can then copy and paste those questions into a Word or Google document and start fleshing out the answers.

If I feel unsure at any point about how to answer, I can ask the AI to help me out further. For example, I could say:

Thanks! How can I work out my "Competitive Advantage: What sets your company apart from competitors?"

Here was the response:

Great question! Determining your company's competitive advantage involves analysing what makes you unique and why customers would choose your services over others. Here are some steps you can take to identify and articulate your competitive advantage:

Identify Your Strengths

1. *Core Competencies: What are the unique capabilities or expertise that your company has?*

2. *Innovative Solutions: Do you offer any cutting-edge products or services that your competitors don't?*

3. **Customer Relationships:** *How strong and positive are your relationships with clients? Do you have a strong reputation for customer service?*

Analyse Your Market

1. **Competitor Analysis:** *Look at your competitors and identify their strengths and weaknesses.*
2. **Market Needs:** *Understand the current demands and pain points of your target market.*
3. **Industry Trends:** *Stay informed about emerging trends in your industry and how your company is positioned to capitalize on them.*

Highlight Your Unique Selling Proposition (USP)

1. **Quality and Performance:** *Is your product or service of higher quality or better performance?*
2. **Pricing Strategy:** *Do you offer better value for the money?*
3. **Brand Image:** *What does your brand stand for, and how does it resonate with your audience?*

Gather Feedback

1. **Customer Testimonials:** *What do your customers love about your company?*
2. **Employee Insights:** *Your employees may have valuable perspectives on what makes your company special.*
3. **Industry Recognition:** *Any awards or recognitions that highlight your company's excellence.*

Summarise Your Findings

Once you've gathered and analysed this information, you can summarise your competitive advantages. For example:

1. **Innovative Training Methods:** *HumanEdge AI Training uses proprietary AI algorithms to personalise training*

> *programs for each client, ensuring higher engagement and effectiveness.*
> 2. ***Exceptional Client Support:*** *We pride ourselves on our dedicated support team that provides 24/7 assistance to our clients.*
> 3. ***Industry Expertise:*** *With over a decade of experience in AI training, we have a deep understanding of the industry's needs and challenges.*
>
> *By taking these steps, you can clearly articulate what sets HumanEdge AI Training apart from competitors and effectively communicate this to potential clients. Does this approach resonate with you?'*

Oh, I always appreciate that question at the end – even though I'm sure many overlook it. By asking, "Does this approach resonate with you?" it hands control back over to the human to consider the information provided and respond accordingly.

Anyway, this type of output is very helpful because it encourages you to think deeper about things. And they could be things you've never thought about before. It's a perfect example of how AI can actually enhance critical and creative thinking instead of replacing it.

After you have all your answers, insert the essential bits and pieces into your AI message bar with this prompt:

> *Thank you. Please see below for everything you need to know about <insert business your name> and provide a summary to confirm you now understand my company. Please remember this information about <insert your business name> for future projects.*

How'd you go? To make things easier for you, I've created a full prompt guide on everything included within this book. Grab your prompt guide from the online resources via the QR code or link on page vi.

Test to check

Now that you've trained your tool about your business, I recommend checking to see if the bot actually "got it". The best way to do this? Give it a task that requires business context!

Here are some sample prompts to experiment with:

Service/Product breakdown

Now that you're familiar with our business, <insert business name>, please explain our core services/products in simple terms. For each one, describe what it is, who it's for and the key benefits it provides. Keep the explanation clear and concise, as if you were explaining it to someone unfamiliar with our industry. Thank you.

One-page business plan

Now that you're familiar with our business, <insert business name>, please draft a one-page business plan summarising our mission, core services/products, target audience, unique value proposition, and key business goals for the next 12 months. Ensure it reflects our industry and competitive positioning while maintaining a professional and strategic tone. Thank you.

Client email draft

Now that you're familiar with our business, <insert business name>, please draft a professional yet personable email to a potential client who has expressed interest in our services. The email should introduce our business, highlight how we can solve their key challenges based on their industry, and include a compelling call to action for a meeting or next steps. Keep the

tone warm and engaging while maintaining professionalism.
Thank you.

Did it nail it or miss the mark? If you think something is missing, here's your opportunity to spark a conversation with your "junior assistant". Yep, with a real human you'd offer corrections or ask questions, so that's what you need to do here. Tell it what it did right and what it did wrong. This all helps with the training, and your future self will thank you.

So, you can reply with prompts like, "Thank you. This is perfect!" or, "Thanks, but the section about <insert incorrect information> is wrong: the product is actually <insert correct information>".

And just continue with that process.

Behind the scenes with AI

For full transparency, I literally had a "correcting" conversation with ChatGPT to suggest the prompts above for you to experiment with. This was my prompt:

Hello! I'd like your help coming up with 3 × AI prompts for a business executive to experiment with after training their AI tool about their business to test whether the tool has a good grasp on the information provided. I'm thinking one prompt could request 5 × social media posts and another could request a one-page business plan. I'm open to other examples that would be suitable for a variety of roles/industries.

When I wasn't satisfied with the initial results provided, I pushed it a bit further:

I'm liking (options) 2 and 3, but I want to replace the social media post one with something that doesn't require brand voice as that will be covered in the next chapter.

Sometimes you don't know what you don't want until you receive the output. And as you can see, while it was in my initial prompt, I ended up omitting the social media example from this section completely. It took a couple more prompts from me to end up with the three prompts featured in this chapter, but we got there! (See the full "transcript" from my conversation in the *AI-Human Fusion* online resources. Please use the QR code or link provided on page vi.)

What if something changes within our business?

The good news is, AI technology itself is ever-evolving – so the tools are completely used to change. At any point, if a new product or service is added or your style guide is updated, simply upload them to your AI with a prompt like these:

We've added a new product/service to <insert business name>. Here's everything you need to know: <Paste information or attach document>. Please remember this information going forward.

Here's the updated style guide for <insert business name>. Please forget the old one previously shared. <Attach document>

My business HumanEdge AI Training has been through a fair few changes over the last couple of years as I've found my feet in this new space. I just keep an eye on the output and, if anything seems misaligned with my current direction, I make updates via prompts like these as needed.

15-minute action step

Today, I want you to try the following:

- Upload your business details (mission, vision, values, key services) to your AI tool.
- Ask the AI to summarise your business in three sentences. Does it sound accurate?
- Test its knowledge by asking for an elevator pitch or a one-page business plan.
- Refine as needed by giving corrections, just like you would to a new team member.

The goal? Ensure your AI tool performs tasks more effectively due to clearly understanding your business.

Final thoughts...

You've now officially started the onboarding process with your AI, meaning you're well on your way to establishing a strong foundation.

As you continue to use your AI and generate more and more output, the tool will get a firmer grasp on your business, meaning the quality will continue to improve. In the following chapters, I cover brand voice and customers, which will result in further improvements.

AI-generated chapter summary *(with human tweaks)*

- The onboarding process is a non-negotiable step in getting quality results from AI tools like ChatGPT, Copilot and Gemini.

- Large language models (LLMs) are pre-trained on vast amounts of data, but they don't know anything about your specific business – until you teach them.

- Without proper onboarding, AI will produce generic, one-size-fits-all output that lacks alignment with your brand voice, strategy and customer needs.

- Key business details to provide:
  - Company overview (mission, vision, values, USP)
  - Products/services breakdown
  - Target audience insights
  - Brand voice/style guidelines (if available).

- No style guide? No problem. AI can help you create one by asking structured questions.

- Test AI's learning by asking it to summarise your services or draft a business plan.

- Update AI as your business evolves to keep outputs relevant.

Chapter 6

Nailing Your Brand Voice

"If you don't sound like you or your brand,
who do you sound like? If you sound like everyone else
out there, you're making it hard for your
customers to remember you."

Angela Pickett

It's Monday morning and you check your email inbox. There are two (at least!) marketing emails waiting for you. One is from Apple, written in a sleek, confident and visionary tone, creating excitement about the latest phone about to hit the stores. The other is from another brand you like... but the wording sounds like it was written by a corporate robot – bland, forgettable and void of personality. Which email are you more likely to pay attention to and remain on the mailing list for?

In early 2024, I was looking for a new mentor – someone who could help me expand my new AI training venture and tap into a world beyond the solopreneurs I'd been hanging out with to date. One of my contacts referred me to a business coach who seemed to really know her stuff. Before making my decision, I started browsing her website and was instantly annoyed. She had all these downloads with business tips and advice – and every single one of them was obviously AI-generated. Trust. Destroyed. I'm sure she's extremely knowledgeable, but as soon as I picked up the lack of effort in her words, I wasn't pursuing the opportunity any further. It was too hard to determine where the AI-generated content ended and where her human brain entered.

Training your AI tools to understand your company's (or your own) brand voice is massively important for maintaining authenticity and trust. And if you don't train your AI to get it right, your content will blend into the sea of generic AI-generated noise. While brand voice isn't as vital when requesting internal strategies and plans for you and your colleagues' eyes only, the moment those words leave your business and enter the public domain – especially for current or potential customers, contractors, resellers or retailers – you need to be certain that the *way* your business is represented really speaks to your audience. This includes emails, phone and video scripts, articles and LinkedIn social media posts. Not training up your tool on your brand voice is one of the biggest mistakes I see out there in the business world. Even AI "experts" are guilty of doing it (much to my surprise).

Hear from the humans
Julia Baker, freelance writer

Brand voice is something that is so deep and personal and I wonder how AI could emulate that in a wholesome, genuine way. I know the word "authentic" is overused, but I think even if AI is used to create branded content, a human must still work on it to ensure you get that authentic feeling and lived experience.

In terms of reading other people's content where you can tell that they have used AI, it's a real turn-off for me. I want to read and feel and connect.

What *is* a brand voice?

If you're a marketer or copywriter, you probably live and breathe this stuff. For everyone else, let me break it down for you. To put it simply, **brand voice is the unique personality your business uses to communicate**. It includes your tone of voice, which is the specific way you convey your brand voice via words in different contexts, the style you use and the way you make people feel when they interact with you.

Here are some examples of words you would use to define the tone of a brand voice:

- Authoritative
- Casual
- Confident
- Enthusiastic
- Formal

- Humorous
- Inspirational
- Professional
- Sarcastic
- Sympathetic

In most cases, you'd use a blend of words to create something unique to your business. For example, when I was experimenting with the development of brand voice for a one-on-one AI training client, we realised we needed a mix of five words to get it right. You might also change these words around for different situations, like soothing a disgruntled client in an email versus creating a sense of FOMO (fear of missing out) or curiosity in a social media advertisement.

There are some great brand voices out there. My favourites include the following:

- **Who Gives a Crap.** I'd honestly love to be a copywriter for these guys who produce subscription-based, sustainable toilet paper. The brand voice is cheeky (pun intended) and light-hearted, breaking down the awkwardness and building relatability of their product. E.g. 'Your bum is a hero. You should get it a cape'.

- **Virgin.** I always have a little giggle when I see signage around the local Virgin Active gym where my youngest does swimming lessons. Its brand voice is cheeky, confident and unafraid to disrupt the status quo. It also stands out in often-serious situations, encouraging people to think differently. E.g. 'Screw it, let's do it.'
- **Red Bull.** While I don't touch the stuff, this energy drink's brand voice uses high-energy, adrenaline-packed language that appeals to thrill-seekers and go-getters. E.g. 'If it scares you, you should probably do it.'

Of course, there are more serious brand voices out there too:

- **Apple.** While I'm an Android user, I appreciate Apple's sleek, sophisticated and visionary brand voice. Concise and to the point, it focuses on how its products fit seamlessly into its users' lives while showcasing its cutting-edge technology. E.g. 'The future of health is on your wrist.'
- **BMW.** Confident, refined and aspirational, the BMW brand voice reflects the company's position as a luxury car manufacturer. Its messaging often centres around performance, craftsmanship and status. E.g. 'The Ultimate Driving Machine'.
- **National Geographic.** This long-standing magazine (which my late Grandpop was a massive fan of) has a brand voice that's authoritative yet awe-inspiring, reflecting its commitment to education, exploration and conservation. The tone often combines scientific accuracy with emotional storytelling. E.g. 'Furthering the understanding and protection of our planet'.

What's your company's brand voice? How does it stand out compared to that of your competitors? Up until now, it's probably been neglected in your brand style guide. But when it comes to AI, its relevance has never been more important.

Hear from the humans
Rachel Amies, WordPress Designer & SEO Copywriter at Crazy Digital Creative

Brand voice isn't just window-dressing or a term that's thrown out there for the hell of it. Brand voice allows potential clients to get a sense of a brand or business owner. If you're clearly using AI-generated content, how can I trust you if I can't sense who you really are? How do I know if your brand's values align with mine?

It's important to 'show up' online regularly. And this can be overwhelming for many business owners. But using bland AI-generated content without personality won't convince me to buy from you. It sticks out like a sore thumb. I used to get a tad angry when I saw AI-generated content. Now, it makes me sad, especially when I know the person who's used it. They're not highlighting their uniqueness.

Another way of looking at this: if you wouldn't send a robot to a business networking event, why let one write your content? Your human touch, your experiences and your values are irreplaceable. And that's what helps you sell your "thing".

Why is brand voice so important?

If you've ever used a copywriter, content marketer or ghostwriter to write your website copy, articles, brochures or thought-leadership books in the past, I'd like you to think about one of the key, overarching, highly-desired outcomes, which was likely to be... drum roll, please... producing words that sounded like they were written by you or match the business's brand voice. Am I right?

Yeah, yeah, you also want the content to be well-structured, engaging, SEO-friendly and likely to convert into sales at some point. Of course. But this highly desired outcome to somehow sound *exactly* like the way you speak, or *exactly* like all the previously written materials your company has pumped out, is a major factor. The importance of getting this right has actually stopped potential clients from working with my copywriting agency in the past. I was told they simply couldn't see how someone else could get into their head and craft content in their brand voice.

After running a successful agency for a decade, I can tell you that it *is* possible. And around the halfway mark in my business, I worked out that the traditional written briefs just weren't working for me or my clients. After all, in most cases, writing wasn't their strong point, which is why they sought a copywriter in the first place! So, I shifted to one-hour Zoom meetings in which the passion for their business and offerings simply poured out of them with only minor prompting from me. One-sentence responses in a written brief became this beautifully expanded monologue – all in their brand voice.

And guess what? Ninety percent of the time my clients were absolutely stoked with the website or article content written as a result. Because it sounded like them. Because we literally used the words that came out of their mouths, then gave it some structure and SEO!

With my business pivot into the AI training space more established, I've now let go of my copywriting agency. But the ghosts of these brand voice experiences still haunt me. It's why it bothers me so much when I see professionals and leaders turning to free or cheap AI tools to write their content for them – without a second thought about the brand voice.

Can you see how ironic it is? In the past, ensuring words produced by an expert copywriter sounded like them was super important. In many cases, it was one of the factors that got in the way of project continuation or sign-off:

Oh, I wouldn't use that word or phrase.

Where did you get that information from? It doesn't sound like me.

With the launch of GenAI, it feels like so many people have forgotten about brand voice. And one of the biggest "icks" of AI-generated content (for everyone I speak to, not just me) is how generic it sounds. Without any effort, this content sounds like absolutely everyone else.

No one in business wants to blur into the background. We all want to stand out and be unique. In marketing speak, we want to highlight our USP to the world. We want to shout out, "We are different from the rest. You should choose us, and this is why...". Nurturing a consistent brand voice is also important for client relationships. You want your website copy, social media posts, articles and videos to reflect the humans who show up at client meetings and networking events.

So, if you're going to embrace AI to replace the role of a copywriter, you need to ensure it's representing you and/or the business well. Because if you just let it take control and write in whatever stock standard voice it's been programmed to do, your clients are going to notice. And they *are* noticing.

If you can't yet tell if something has been written by AI, trust me, you will. As a human copywriter who's been hanging out in the AI space for more than two years now, I can spot untrained content from 10 km away. My spidey senses start tingling as soon as it scrolls by my screen. And I'm getting more and more annoyed by it. Especially when I see AI enthusiasts, who should know better, making this mistake.

People are following them, trusting them to be conducting best practices when it comes to AI. But it's become clear that too many of them are caught up in the "productivity" of it all. Or, they are so overwhelmed about keeping up with the fast-paced changes in this space that they think they don't have time to take care with their content. But here's the secret: if you spend the time now to undergo this whole training process, you'll save so much more time in the long run.

This is why training your AI tools to understand and replicate your brand voice should be one of the first core steps you take – right after you train it up to understand your business. However, if you don't know, you don't know.

As I'm writing these words, AI tools aren't prioritising brand voice enough. This is why I tell my students to ignore all the programs and software that have jumped onto the AI bandwagon, acting like Microsoft's "Clippy" character from the 1990s: "It looks like you're writing an email. Would you like some help?"

None of these tools ask for the brand voice you'd like to write in. They all just do whatever the hell they want based on what they were pre-trained to do by their engineer. Until these tools can be integrated with one main tool – the tool you've trained to understand your business and voice – I don't recommend using them. The messaging will be inconsistent with everything else you mindfully produce via your LLM or GenAI of choice. And you don't want that, because others will pick up on it. Sure, you can go back and tweak the copy to make it sound more like you. But at some point in time, when you're tired after a long day and just want that email sent, it will be very easy to just click "Send" instead of proofreading the AI-generated content.

And that's a trap I encourage you to avoid.

> ## Hear from the humans
> *Laura Mudge, Digital Marketing Consultant*

I feel like I can spot AI from a mile off these days, especially for brands and businesses I know, and it just doesn't match up.

Full transparency, I'm using AI a lot to help me with writing now as it's made me so much more efficient with my time. I never use it as it is – even when it's working with my own words and work.

It absolutely has a place, but you really need to invest time into learning how to use it and also then to teach it to get the quality output.

Let's have a bit of fun here. I want to show you, from the following short activity, the massive difference you can make when you include variations of tone of voice in your prompting.

Activity: Varying your voice

Head over to your Generative AI of choice – e.g. ChatGPT, Copilot, Gemini – and type:

> *Please write a 500-word article about the importance of brand voice in AI-generated content.*

Obviously, you can insert any topic of your choosing here, but just go with me for a moment. Have a read through the output received. If you've done absolutely no training with your tool, the content is likely to be extremely generic, robotic and lifeless. Because it's been given no clear direction from the human, the bot just does whatever the hell it wants. It's most likely to be written in a professional tone suitable for a white paper, because these tools have been heavily trained on white papers.

For the next step, I want you to type:

> *Thank you. Please rewrite this article in a professional and conversational tone of voice.*

How does the output change? You're likely to see more relaxed wording and feel a different vibe. However, the overall message is likely to be the same.

Then try:

Thank you. Please rewrite this article in a professional, conversational and quirky tone of voice.

You'll now see a playful element enter the content. The words and energy will have changed, but once again, the message remains the same. Pretty cool, yeah? Imagine how the quality will improve even more after training your tool on your business, brand voice *and* target market. (The last part is coming up in the next chapter, so stay tuned...)

If this is a new concept to you, I bet you're having a massive *mind blown* or *a-ha* moment right now. This is one of those major gold nuggets I love to share!

How do you make your AI-generated content sound like you?

After using ChatGPT fairly consistently for more than two years now, the tool seems to have worked out my business's brand voice (although, on many occasions, this has been the result of regular reminders from me...). The other day, I literally spent an hour on a thought-leadership article in collaboration with AI, which would have otherwise taken me at least twice the time if writing from scratch. The final piece was about 80% AI-generated – however, it wound up sounding exactly like me. It didn't happen by accident. It was thanks to the saved "memory" of previous content in my brand voice, fine-tuning my prompts, and critiquing.

Smashing it out in only an hour meant I could save my energy for working on this book – something that truly matters to me. The hour saved went towards writing this chapter, actually!

So, how do you ensure your AI-generated content produces similar results? While it will take some time and training to build up your tool to the same position as mine, it's vital to lay down strong foundations. I want to emphasise that it's *not* just a matter of sharing with your AI the three to five words used to describe your brand voice in your style guide. *Why not?* Because the human perception of brand voice could very well differ from AI's perception. While your marketing team believes the words "professional, sophisticated and approachable" are perfectly aligned with what you're trying to achieve, the GenAI tool mightn't agree.

So, what do you do? Oh, I'm glad you asked!

I recommend the following process:

1. Source three or four examples of your company's content that nail your brand voice with regard to wording and energy. They could be pieces that have attracted a lot of online engagement or that your colleagues feel aligned with. These could be articles, long-form social media posts or webpages.

2. Open up your GenAI tool and paste the words, or insert links to them, in the message bar.

3. Insert the following prompt:

    Here are samples of content from my company, <insert company name>. Could you please review the company's brand voice, structure and writing style? Then, create a writing style guide with the core headings. <Insert samples here>

    Review the output and see if you agree. I then recommend testing it out in the same chat session to see if it hits the mark. Your follow up prompt could be something like:

This is sounding good, but I think it needs to be more <approachable/sophisticated/casual, etc.>. Could you please try again?

Remember to treat it like your (human) junior assistant. What would you say to them to achieve what you want to achieve?

15-minute action step

Today, I want you to try the following:

- Upload three or four brand voice samples (e.g. social posts, blogs or website copy) to your AI tool.
- Ask your AI to analyse and summarise your brand voice into three to five key traits.
- Test it by asking it to write a social media post or email using your brand voice.
- Refine as needed by giving corrections, just as you would with a new employee.

The goal? Ensure your AI-generated content sounds like your brand – not a generic bot.

Final thoughts...

I bet you're thinking about all your AI-generated content to date in a completely different way now. And that makes my heart sing, because it's one of the core goals I aim to achieve with my clients in both team and one-on-one AI training.

If you follow this process, it will set you apart from the large proportion of the world's population who are either ignorant or completely blasé about the importance of brand voice in their AI-generated content. But you're not one of them now. You have this power to ensure generic, robotic, lifeless content is a thing of the past for your organisation. That means you're more likely to maintain integrity and that "know, like and trust" factor with your clients who are otherwise sick of seeing AI-written crap. Hooray for you!

AI-generated chapter summary *(with human tweaks)*

- Brand voice is the unique personality your business uses to communicate and connect with your audience. It encompasses tone, vocabulary and the emotional resonance of your content.

- AI tools can be used internally (e.g. for strategy development) or externally (e.g. to write customer-facing materials). Internal use requires less concern with tone, while external use demands consistency with your brand voice.

- Failing to train AI tools on your brand voice results in generic and robotic content that can damage authenticity and customer trust.

- Successful brand voices include Red Bull (high-energy and daring), Apple (sophisticated and sleek) and National Geographic (authoritative and awe-inspiring). These examples highlight the impact of a well-crafted voice.

- Training AI to match your brand voice involves sharing samples of your existing content, refining outputs and briefing AI as if it were a human assistant.

- Adjusting the tone in AI-generated content can produce very different results. For example, you can experiment with tones like professional, conversational or quirky to align with specific goals.

Chapter 7

Considering Your Audience

*"If your AI doesn't understand your business
and customer pain points, it's useless."*

Anfernee Chanasmooth

With the flurry of AI enthusiasm in the world, it would be very easy for me as an AI trainer to get swept up with it all. I admit there have been countless times when I've wondered whether I "should" be talking about the latest tools and updates. I mean, that's what all the other AI enthusiasts are doing.

But then I think about my audience of busy, overwhelmed leaders. Yes, that's you. What do you actually need from me right now? You're not seeking more shiny things to confuse or frustrate you. You're seeking solutions that speak to your issues (aka pain points). You want to move away from feeling unprepared, unclear and unskilled with AI. Instead, you want to feel prepared, purposeful and progressive to reach the golden calf of "productivity". And you want to keep everything human-centred. Because nobody wants the bots to completely take over.

See? I get you. I keep in mind all of your emotional and mental turmoil, as well as your goals for effective human-first AI implementation, when producing my online content, workshops and keynotes – and, of course, while working on this book. Because that's what you're looking for.

It then feels so rewarding when I receive direct messages from new LinkedIn connections like Kirstie, who says:

> *So relieved to have come across you and your work. You are the very first person in the AI field here on LinkedIn that seems to have an approach to AI that resonates with my personal and professional values.*

Heartfelt comments like Kirstie's remind me that I'm on the right track with my messaging and purpose. My core messages are resonating with my audience – and I intend to keep it that way. Especially when I choose to use AI to support me with content creation.

From your experimentation with GenAI so far, you're now seeing a huge difference in the quality of output, right? This is what happens when you take the time to introduce background context. The quality will only continue to improve when you move on to the third key aspect of the onboarding process: teaching it about your audience (aka your ideal target market). Because if you don't cover this aspect, all your efforts will fall flat. You'll just wind up sounding like all your competitors.

Sure, the tool knows all about you and the company now, but you can't run a successful business without considering the people you're serving. You also need absolute clarity on who you are serving. This information must be included in the onboarding process so your GenAI tool knows how to support you with building effective systems, processes, strategies and content. Your audience is everything, so you can't forget about them.

You might have absolute clarity on who these people are. If that's so, you need to ensure your AI tool has an equal or higher level of clarity to get it right – or at least be on a fairly close track so you can guide further if necessary. Confused about who you really want to work with? With the right prompts, your AI tool can step in to help. That includes all you enthusiastic entrepreneurs out there who've worked with anyone with a pulse to date and been scarred on many occasions. With AI support, you can move past that mindset and be on your way to earning the big bucks from those you value and those who show appreciation in return.

Why keep the audience in mind?

Unfortunately, I think many leaders and professionals forget about their target market when working with AI. As mentioned previously, it's just so easy to get caught up in how AI can serve you and your team for productivity reasons – and lose track of how the output could be negatively absorbed by outsiders. Today's consumers are highly sensitive to inauthenticity. If they feel like they're reading something soulless and generic, they'll quickly disengage. I know that's what I do!

Think about those lifeless, templated LinkedIn posts or DMs that completely ignore who you are and what you do. I've heard many examples of SEO consultants receiving pitches for SEO services, website developers receiving pitches for website services, and so on. We all know it's so easy to copy and paste a generic message and spam a bunch of people. And it's so easy to pay an offshore virtual assistant to proceed with the task, no questions asked. But unless some real work has been put into understanding your audience, it's all a waste of time. We'll talk a bit more about the social media side in Chapter 9: Relationships, Recognition and Revenue.

In summary, having clarity around your audience isn't optional. It's essential.

Speaking as a marketer, I know ignoring the people I'm selling to is a big no-no. I need to be listening to their pain points, needs, wants and dreams. I then need to offer suggestions and solutions that truly meet them where they're at. Only then will they listen to me, follow me and want to invest in me. So, while it's all well and good to pump out AI-generated content that cleverly represents your business and brand voice, if the message doesn't land, and if you're not making it clear how you can help others, it's just not going to work the way you hope. They'll wind up feeling misunderstood, thinking you don't care. And that's the last thing you want!

Keeping your audience in mind is also essential for building smooth and effective internal systems, processes and strategies with AI. It ensures everything is customised and the cogs all work together to achieve desirable results. For example, say you manage a hospitality group that operates both a five-star luxury hotel and a budget-friendly business hotel. You've got two different types of customer persona here: luxury travellers, who are high-net-worth individuals and executives, and budget-conscious business travellers.

If you ask AI to write a social media ad without audience details, you might get something vague like:

Book your next stay with us – comfort and convenience guaranteed!

Very generic, right? But after some training, your AI is more likely to produce something like this for luxury travellers:

Indulge in unparalleled elegance. From private butler service to Michelin-star dining, experience five-star luxury designed for discerning travellers. Reserve your suite today and elevate your next business trip or holiday.

… And this for budget-conscious business travellers:

Maximise productivity without maxing out your budget. Stay in the heart of the city with high-speed wi-fi, flexible workspaces and affordable comfort. Book your stay now!

In each of these examples, the words are speaking to the audience's pain points and desires. Generic messaging just won't draw the right people in. As they say, if you try to speak to everyone, you end up speaking to no one.

Hear from the humans
Anfernee Chanasmooth, Marketing Coach at Authentic Marketer

A doctor wouldn't prescribe meds without a diagnosis after asking the patient what's wrong, and a builder wouldn't build a house without a plan informed by speaking with the homeowner and architect. AI is no different – if it doesn't get your audience, it's just generating noise. Yet, businesses keep using AI content verbatim. If everyone does that, how do you stand out? Google's also burying content that lacks real expertise.

You need to challenge AI's output. Ask, how are we different? What do we actually know about our customers, and how do we truly solve their problems? Train it with real customer data and proof of experience. AI should support your strategy, not replace your thinking.

Training our GenAI to 'know' our target market

For those of you with communication and brand style guides, someone has likely gone to the effort of establishing customer personas or avatars for your company – in other words, a profile of your ideal client including key characteristics, primary challenges and desired solutions. They usually have a pretend name and age, and a stock or AI-generated photo of what they look like. The intention behind this mock person is to give you an imaginary person to consider when making decisions within your role, whatever that may be.

So, if you have two or three (or more!) of these customer personas, you need to share them with your GenAI tool. This is actually fairly simple to do. Just paste them into the message bar and provide a prompt like:

> *Here are our <insert number> customer personas for*
> *<insert business name>. Please remember these.*

That should do the job. But then you can test it by returning to the conversation you had with your AI tool for the "Varying your voice" activity in the previous chapter. Choose one of the personas and insert the following prompt:

> *Please rewrite this article with the customer persona of*
> *<insert pretend name> in mind. Ensure the content speaks to*
> *their pain points and presents our company's perspectives and*
> *solutions in a way they'd understand.*

Watch how the article shifts its perspective. Pretty cool, huh? You can repeat the process for the other customer personas as well. And, of course, you can experiment with other tasks like emails or proposals you've been procrastinating about all week.

Hear from the humans
Bridget Holland, Director at NoBull Marketing

What happens if AI doesn't know the pain points of your audience? Same as what happens when your marketing team or agency don't know the pain points of your audience. You produce marketing materials which do not engage or interest your audience. AI simply lets you produce more of it, faster.

On the other hand, if you know the pain points of your audience and you teach your AI those pain points, it can produce effective marketing content which hits home with your audience (or at least first drafts) far more quickly than most humans. It can also do great things like come up with 10 or 20 hook lines for you to pick and choose between, or to use as inspiration for one you craft yourself.

Crafting customer personas

If you've never gone through the process of establishing customer personas, then it's AI to the rescue! However, the following tips I'm sharing will only be effective if you've already trained the tool on your company background. So, if you've skipped that step, I recommend popping back to Chapter 5: Briefing the Bot About Your Business.

Here's a prompt for you to try:

With everything you know about <insert company name>, please describe one of our ideal customers, including their key characteristics, primary challenges and what they are looking for in a solution. Then, outline how our business specifically addresses their needs and differentiates itself from competitors. Please give them a name, age and role, plus other demographic details. Thank you.

You can then repeat the prompt a couple of times to see what else you get. Ideally, you would have already provided an indication of who you serve as part of the business outline. From this prompt, you're seeking details to make your target market come to life.

Because my ChatGPT knows HumanEdge AI Training so well, it delivered me incredible results. Let's have a look at some of the summarised personas it drafted for me.

Meet David Carter – The Time-Strapped Business Executive

Age: 48 | *Role:* CEO | *Industry:* Professional services | *Team Size:* 50-200 employees

AI Usage: Minimal – sees AI's value but hasn't implemented it effectively

Challenges:

1. *No Time to Learn AI* – Needs fast, high-level insights without getting stuck in technical details.
2. *Competitive Pressure* – Worries about falling behind competitors already using AI.
3. *Skeptical About AI Replacing Humans* – Wants AI to support decision-making, not replace expertise.
4. *Unclear How AI Can Solve Business Problems* – Needs a practical adoption roadmap.
5. *Team Resistance & Buy-In Issues* – Mixed attitudes toward AI within leadership and staff.

How HumanEdge AI Training Helps:

- *Executive-Friendly AI Training* – Concise, no-nonsense insights on AI's business impact.
- *AI Strategy Roadmap* – Clear, step-by-step integration plan tailored to his industry.
- *Enhancing Human Leadership with AI* – Helps drive efficiency without losing human expertise.
- *Leadership & Team Alignment* – Smooth AI adoption with structured team education.
- *Tangible Business Benefits* – AI-use cases that save time, reduce costs, and improve decision-making.

How We Stand Out: We cut through the AI noise with practical, high-impact training designed for busy executives who need fast, actionable results.

Meet Jessica Reynolds – The Ambitious Marketing Agency Owner

Age: 38 | *Role:* Founder & Director |
Industry: Marketing & advertising | *Team Size:* 8-12

AI Usage: Intermediate – her team uses AI inconsistently, leading to inefficiencies

Challenges:

1. *Balancing AI Efficiency & Creativity* – Needs AI workflows that enhance, not dilute, quality.
2. *Scaling Without Overloading Her Team* – Wants AI to boost productivity without burnout.
3. *Clients Are Asking About AI* – Needs the right messaging to position her agency as AI-savvy.
4. *AI Usage is Inconsistent Across Her Team* – Lacks a structured, agency-wide approach.
5. *Standing Out in a Competitive Market* – Must prove the value of human expertise alongside AI.

How HumanEdge AI Training Helps:

- ✅ *Marketing-Focused AI Training* – AI workflows built for content, branding, and strategy.
- ✅ *Scalable AI-Enhanced Workflows* – Increases agency efficiency while keeping content high-quality.
- ✅ *Guidance on Client AI Conversations* – Helps position her agency as an AI-savvy thought leader.
- ✅ *Team-Wide AI Adoption Plan* – Standardised AI processes to ensure quality control and efficiency.
- ✅ *AI-Powered Business Growth* – Helps her integrate AI into services, pricing, and client strategies.

How We Stand Out: Unlike generic AI training, we offer agency-specific strategies that help scale without losing creativity, quality, or brand differentiation.

Meet Daniel Foster – The Growth-Focused Entrepreneur

Age: 35 | *Role:* Founder & CEO | *Industry:* Business consulting | *Team Size:* 3 full-time + contractors

AI Usage: Beginner – has experimented with AI but hasn't fully integrated it

Challenges:

1. *Wearing Too Many Hats* – Needs AI to streamline content, admin, and productivity.
2. *Inconsistent Content Creation* – Struggles to maintain a strong online presence.
3. *Limited AI Knowledge* – Unsure how to apply AI beyond basic ChatGPT use.
4. *Maintaining a Personal Brand* – Wants AI to support, not dilute, his unique voice.
5. *Scaling Without Burnout* – Needs AI to increase efficiency without over-reliance.

How HumanEdge AI Training Helps:

- ✅ *AI for Business Growth* – Practical AI strategies that save time and increase productivity.
- ✅ *Content Creation with Authenticity* – AI-powered blog, LinkedIn, and email workflows.
- ✅ *Smart Automations* – AI tools that reduce admin without losing personal engagement.
- ✅ *Clear, No-Jargon Approach* – Actionable AI training without complexity or fluff.
- ✅ *Ongoing AI Support* – Continuous learning to keep him ahead of AI trends.

How We Stand Out: Tailored AI training for entrepreneurs who need efficiency, growth, and AI-driven content—without losing their personal touch.

Based on general conversations I've had with clients in the past, these seem to be pretty spot-on. But I can now manually change the draft personas provided or offer corrections via follow-up prompts. Once finalised, ask your AI to save it to memory:

Thank you. Here are the final customer personas for <insert company name>. Please remember these for future projects.

I recommend saving them somewhere else too. Potentially, you could use them to kick off that style guide you've been meaning to establish.

15-minute action step

Today, I want you to try the following:
- Upload at least one customer persona to your AI tool.
- Test it by having AI rewrite an email or blog post for that persona.
- Compare the new version to a generic version. Notice the difference?

The goal? Have a bigger impact on your audience by developing content that truly speaks to their pain points and desires.

Activity – developing content pillars

Now that you've trained your GenAI to understand your business and audience, you have the perfect opportunity to fuse both your service and product offerings with your clients' needs by establishing content pillars or themes.

What type of content would your audience associate with the best? What's going to keep them engaged, interacting, following and eventually buying from you?

Here's a prompt to experiment with:

Based on everything you know about our business and customers, what are five suitable content pillars for my business?

Final thoughts...

Congratulations! That concludes the formal onboarding of your AI junior assistant.

You're now ahead of about 90% of the population. Over the coming weeks, I encourage you to experiment with various day-to-day tasks within your GenAI tool and critically review the output. I bet if you compare it to everything you've generated to date, it will be leaps and bounds ahead.

AI-generated chapter summary *(with human tweaks)*

- Audience clarity is key. AI tools, like ChatGPT, Copilot and Gemini, will generate generic and ineffective content if they aren't trained on your ideal customers.

- Failing to consider the audience leads to disconnect. Many professionals focus on how AI serves them internally (e.g. with productivity, automation) but forget that AI-generated customer-facing materials must resonate with the audience. Poorly aligned content risks sounding robotic, impersonal or irrelevant.

- Well-defined customer personas improve AI output. Just as businesses create personas for marketing and sales strategies, AI needs to be trained with detailed customer profiles, including key characteristics, challenges and pain points.

- Training AI on customer personas is simple. Uploading personas directly into your AI tool allows it to tailor content more effectively.

- AI can also help create personas. If your business lacks clear audience definitions, AI can assist in identifying and refining ideal customer profiles through guided prompts.

- By training AI to recognise your ideal audience, you ensure that all AI-generated content – whether for sales, marketing or customer engagement – sounds relevant, engaging and tailored.

Chapter 8

From Clicks to Conversations

*"We need to concentrate on building strong connections
with others, ideally to make a conversation about them
and not just about us."*

Gunnar Habitz

The week before I wrote this chapter, I had a really enjoyable one-on-one training experience with a new client named Patricia. Since I'm an ADHD woman with an ADHD daughter, and Patricia offers neurodiverse support and education to families, her business piqued my interest from the get-go because, to put it simply, I'm her target audience. (While I've got a handle on my own brain, when it comes to my wild eight-year-old, I'm somewhat out of my depth!)

Towards the end of the three-hour session, after we'd trained her GenAI tool to understand her business, brand voice and customers, we started playing around with the development of social media posts. Now, in the past I haven't seen AI produce the best stuff for social media. In many cases, despite providing plenty of guidance in the prompts – like requests for longer word counts and the addition of emotion – the output was always too short and flat. But the posts we produced with AI support that day actually brought me to tears. They connected with me in many ways. I was nodding my head along with each and every one. I felt that these messages "from" Patricia completely "got me".

As previously mentioned, both you and your GenAI tool need to completely understand your audience to achieve optimal results. And that's what happened with Patricia. Her week's social media posts were sorted. They sounded like her and they connected with her target audience (aka me). What more could you want?

In this chapter, we'll look at some use cases of AI in action for business-to-consumer (B2C) purposes. You'll see how your learnings start to trickle in...

Articles

To put it simply, AI-generated content lacks emotional intuition and energy. The tools simply don't understand the nuances and impact of a heartfelt story shared in an article. Without human guidance, they're likely to deliver lifeless, skeletal articles. The bones of a good message might be there, but there's not enough blood (aka passion) circulating, and the stories haven't been 'fleshed' out.

It's often because the people behind the bots haven't taken the time to add human opinions and remarks, client case studies, facts and figures, and relatable stories. And many are using AI-generated templates or just asking AI to write stuff from a one-line prompt. From my experience, these people either don't know what they don't know, or they've been caught up in AI shiny object syndrome.

This is why I'm so concerned when I hear about whole copywriting and marketing teams being sacked and replaced by AI. It makes me sad, because these are the human experts who know how to produce quality blogs and articles. These are the people who could use what they know to actually optimise AI tools. With the right training on AI tools, their human creativity could go absolutely gangbusters.

After the initial AI onboarding process, you can't just let AI take over. When it comes to producing high-quality articles, I highly recommend conducting old-school research via Google to find credible and reliable sources that maintain a sense of authority. These could be researched articles or reports from industry or government publications, or from trustworthy media sources.

The next step is to start piecing your article together. Here's the strategy I personally use to create high-quality articles via an ethical collaboration between AI and my human brain:

1. Source credible and reliable sources to write the article. These could also include notes from past workshops, keynotes, programs or manuscripts.

2. Ask your GenAI tool to draft an initial outline using a prompt like one of these:

   Hello! I'd like your help in drafting an article in the HumanEdge AI Training brand voice on <insert topic here>. Please refer to the following resources: <insert here>. It needs to be 500 to 700 words long. Could you please provide the outline? OR

   Hello! I'd like your help in drafting an article in the HumanEdge AI Training brand voice on <insert topic here>. I want you to only use the past materials I've provided you from my book, workshops and keynotes. It needs to be 500 to 700 words long. Could you please provide the outline?

3. Review the article outline, then provide positive reinforcement (for training purposes) or request changes as necessary. For example:

   Thank you, this is looking great. But could you please remove the section on <insert here>? I'd like to focus more on <insert preferred topic here>.

4. Confirm the outline is ready and request a draft of the introduction. For example:

    Thank you. Here is the final edited outline for this article. Could you please proceed with drafting the 100- to 150-word introduction? Ensure you maintain the HumanEdge AI Training brand voice at all times. Feel free to use hypothetical or rhetorical questions to create a sense of engagement.

5. Review the initial output and paste it into a Word or Google doc. Make your manual human tweaks – like adding phrases, quotes, facts or stories and removing typical AI-generated phrases – until you're happy. Alternatively, you can have a friendly conversation with your GenAI to make suitable changes. (Warning: this can become frustrating if it just doesn't "get it".) Confirm the changes with the bot, then ask it to proceed with the next section. For example:

    Thank you. Here's the updated introduction. Could you please proceed with writing the following section – once again maintaining our brand voice – and keep it to around 200 words?

6. Continue this process until the article is complete.

While you may need to remind the AI to maintain your brand voice at times, this should help you produce an article that is 90% better than most of the AI-generated content you find online. By keeping across the process from start to finish, alongside your handy technical partner, you can produce a human-centric piece that you're proud to show the world – and that also connects with your audience.

If you need a bit of support with cross-checking your AI-generated article content, check out "Your AI-Humanisation Checklist" in the *AI-Human Fusion* online resources: see the QR code or link provided on page vi.

Bonus tip: for improved quality, you can ask your GenAI tool to "pretend" or "act as" something for content generation. This gives it a lens to work from. For example: "Pretend you are an expert copywriter that specialises in AI", or, "Act as an emotional storyteller".

Experiment with it and see how it changes the output!

Hear from the humans
Raffe Gold, Marketing and Content Strategist at SoJust Solutions

I can be super productive but creatively lazy, and for someone who thrives on storytelling there's no better feeling than finding that one-in-a-million word to add humanity and depth to a sentence.

The ability to work with a creative and technical partner at all times has allowed me to understand more about the specifics of issues – and be far more self-sufficient than I otherwise would have been. It accelerates the first step in how I approach problems, provided I verify everything that it says.

Chatbots

More and more companies are introducing AI chatbots on their website to enhance the customer experience. Personally, I prefer chatting with live humans so I can get a straight answer straight away. But I get it – from a business perspective, AI chatbots are a handy way to save team members from answering the same questions over and over. These bots can be trained to know all your FAQs and other core details that can be found across your marketing materials.

If someone comes to your website with a basic question, which the bot can answer, awesome – they'll leave with a feeling of satisfaction. The problem comes when questions are more complicated. And no one wants to wind up going round and round in circles with a bot when they need a human. It's especially frustrating when there isn't a contact number or email address on the site, either – just a bot and a contact form (that may or may not work).

For an effective experience, chatbots must be set up correctly and ensure the customer remains top of mind at all times. Being transferred to a human for unique and personalised queries needs to be easy. I believe full transparency that the bot is just a bot is also vital. Tala Chisholm from Pivot Point Pty Ltd (who calls herself a 'Chief Chatbot Magician') agrees with me: "The unspoken rule in the world of AI chatbots is never to try to trick the user into thinking the chatbot is a human. Although it's sometimes hard to tell – if the bot is trained well – it's always best practice to make it clear it's a bot having the conversation."

Tala says, like most other services, there are various levels of sophistication in AI chatbots. Some have very limited context, meaning only basic information about the company has been added to the bot's knowledge base. This then needs to be updated manually every time you update your website content or policies: "These tools will be the most affordable option but are unsuitable for businesses where the content changes often, or for those with a large content knowledge base such as e-commerce businesses, education or corporate organisations."

There are other chatbots that can be linked with your website Content Management System (CMS). But Tala says many of those are nothing more than a glorified search bar: "They're merely a search tool that scans the website content and answers direct questions using the answers contained within the website. These can also point users to the URLs where they can find more information about their query."

However, Tala explains there are more sophisticated AI chatbots which can be extensively trained to achieve several business objectives, such as the following:

- **Uncovering the real issues.** Asking dynamic lead-qualification questions based on the user's responses helps the bot understand the inquiry better and point them towards the "best" answer, rather than providing an instant but possibly incorrect answer to a direct question.

- **Capturing lead details at the right time.** Asking the user for their name, email address or contact number, but *only* mid-conversation and without blocking the conversation, improves the customer experience, because users might feel uncomfortable being forced to share their details before they get the chance to ask their question. It's a bit like walking into a hardware store and asking the person at the entrance where you can find the garden hoses, but they refuse to answer you unless you first hand over your name and email address. Most of the time, this process turns customers away or sends them down rabbit holes as they attempt to find answers on their own without your help, causing further frustration.

- **Integrating with customer relationship management (CRM) tools.** You can increase your chances of capitalising on website visitors by instantly adding the conversation and information from chatbot to your CRM. Human staff can then easily follow up via email or phone call, or you can initiate a lead-magnet or first-buyer-discount email sequence.

- **Integrating with helpdesk applications.** This makes it possible to pass the user to a human if needed.

- **Integrating with documents for additional content.** Training the chatbot or linking it up with documents such as product manuals, business policies, shipping rates and handbooks can allow the bot to answer questions already explained elsewhere.

For e-commerce businesses, Tala says integrating with shopping platforms like Shopify, Magento and WooCommerce can yield additional benefits, such as allowing the chatbot to access more detailed product information and stock levels, as well as the user's latest orders to advise them of their status or tracking details. It can also take requests for changes and either make those changes directly within the platform or pass them to the appropriate departments within the business.

According to Tala's experience with several e-commerce businesses, sophisticated AI chatbots have the ability to take over 70% to 80% of front-end website inquiries, which were previously handled by live agents. They also show an increased number of conversations compared to live agent systems (aka human customer service representatives). It means the typical, repetitive questions can be handled by the bots before the humans need to intervene.

A well-trained chatbot that's integrated with a live agent helpdesk will pass the user to a human customer service representative if the user asks to speak to a human, or if the AI detects from the flow of the conversation that the user is not receiving a satisfactory answer to their query. Some sophisticated chatbots will also allow humans to monitor AI and user conversations and initiate a takeover if they see the need.

The more money and time you invest into training the chatbots, the better the result. Just be mindful about replacing the human customer service representatives altogether to avoid possible frustration from the user.

Hear from the humans

Tala Chisholm, Chief Chatbot Magician at Pivot Point Pty Ltd

Choosing the most suitable chatbot option for your situation depends on the complexity of your requirements.

If you have a simple, service-based business where the content rarely changes, a basic AI chatbot would suit you best. Just expect that there will be deficiencies in how far the chatbot can "carry the conversation" and that it's unlikely to be able to smoothly collect CRM info or connect to a helpdesk.

If your content is larger and your user inquiries need a deeper understanding and integration with your website platform, then the more sophisticated chatbots will be better suited to your requirements to offer a real difference in the user experience.

Phone agents

Similar to chatbots, AI phone agents – used for both inbound and outbound calls – can be very handy for providing or collating basic answers. My frustration stems from the AI enthusiasts online who make comments like, "Wow, did you know an AI Phone Agent can make 1,000 calls every second? How cool is that? You don't need a sales team anymore. You can cut your payroll in half!" Ughhhhhh…

Having said that, there are ways to use AI phone agents to keep everyone happy, both internally and externally. I approached Naomi Stockman from My Virtual AI to address this topic. In her virtual receptionist business, her team noticed that 50% of businesses don't usually answer the phone when it rings. If that's a potential client calling for information or to make an appointment, this leads to missed opportunities, inconveniences and possibly brand damage. "If I personally call a business with a question and get an answer, I'm happy," says Naomi. "Customers call for a reason – and if their need is met, they're satisfied and won't go elsewhere."

Think you're sorted because you have voicemail set up? The problem is, in many cases the person calling wants an instant answer. Hearing a voicemail message is like hitting a dead end, meaning they're likely to move on to the next business to call.

Naomi says AI phone agents ensure the call doesn't go to voicemail:

They can take information, book an appointment or convert an inquiry into something actionable. They have a soft sales capacity and can guide the caller to the next step, like saying, "I've taken your details for the quote, and you'll receive it within the next few hours". They can even check stock levels and respond accordingly. With a little planning, the possibilities are incredible.

AI phone agents can make and take unlimited calls simultaneously, making them very effective for scaling. They're also available 24/7 and don't sleep. You can set time conditions too; for example, during business hours, calls can be transferred, but after hours, the AI can take a different action. It's very beneficial for businesses that want to be global, or for those servicing multiple time zones. The interaction is always available. It can take you anywhere you want to go.

I was sceptical about receiving cold calls from a robot, but Naomi says they can actually work really well in certain scenarios, like appointment confirmations:

For example, the script could be something like, "Hi, I'm calling from XYZ. You have an appointment tomorrow for a quote on your new carport. Just confirming you'll be available to meet the technician?" This is very helpful for businesses that send people on site, ensuring someone will be there and reducing the chances of being stood up. AI gives organisations the opportunity to focus on what they do best while AI handles the repetitive tasks.

So, what's the process for training a phone agent? Naomi explains it's very similar to training a new receptionist:

You want them to know specific things, and over time their knowledge grows. For example, if a receptionist comes to you and says, "I had a call about this – what should I say?" you provide the answer, and they learn accordingly. Similarly, with the AI you get to see summaries of all the calls, and it will notify you if it was unable to answer a question. You can then add that information to enhance its knowledge base.

You can also teach the tool scenario-based actions for call transfers, information capture and text messaging. For example, based on the human response to "How can I help you today?" the agent can be trained to ask relevant follow-up questions, then transfer callers to the most suitable department or team member. By the time the call is transferred, the AI can have a summary prepared, including the caller ID and details collected during the interaction:

It's very quick, user-friendly, and doesn't require much technical knowledge. I'm operationally focused and could easily set up a strong working model. I've had a lot of fun playing with the AI, testing and programming it myself. It's fascinating to see what happens when I add or remove something, do another test call and make adjustments. It also integrates with other software, like Zapier, allowing application programming interface (API) hooks and automation. It's very flexible in terms of outcomes.

Would having phone agents be beneficial to your company? Just remember to be completely transparent when utilising them, and never set up and use agents in a way that gives customers the false pretence that they're talking to a human. For example, Naomi's team programs their AI to clearly say it's a digital team member. "Ethics are essential," Naomi says. "With any business tool, you can use it to do the right thing or the wrong thing."

It's also important to note that with the technology constantly advancing, it's unlikely to be a set-and-forget system anytime soon, so be prepared for frequent updates and retraining.

Hear from the humans

Naomi Stockman, Director at My Virtual AI

Businesses that don't answer their phones aren't measuring those lost calls or the potential revenue they've missed. Once the AI is in place, you can track the number of inquiries, where they came from and what they were about. This allows follow-up opportunities, delivers insights and improves conversion rates. It's a game-changer for businesses looking to grow, establish a solid brand, or focus on personalised sales rather than just answering calls.

Trust is built through experiences. A good website builds trust by showcasing credibility. Social platforms and reviews add social proof. When you combine this with great AI technology, followed up by genuine human care, you create a solid foundation. It tells customers, "We're at the forefront of our industry. We're not operating out of a garage – we're a forward-thinking, tech-savvy business".

Final thoughts...

I'm seeing too much focus on efficiency when it comes to using AI for business. It's time for everyone to move to a different frame of reference – how you can positively impact your customers.

Sure, a lot of businesses have done haphazard or rushed implementations which have annoyed customers in the past – you know, like sending all customer service offshore to call centres. But there *is* a way to get it right to ensure customers receive a genuinely improved experience. It's not easy, and it's not quick, but the long-term gains can be massive.

AI-generated chapter summary *(with human tweaks)*

- AI is transforming B2C marketing and customer interactions. Businesses are using AI to create content, enhance customer service and optimise communication channels.

- AI-generated content lacks emotional depth. Without human input, AI-produced articles and social media posts can feel flat, missing the storytelling and relatability needed to engage audiences. When guided with structured prompts and human oversight, AI-generated content can be aligned with brand voice and audience expectations.

- AI chatbots improve customer service. Well-trained bots can handle FAQs, qualify leads and integrate with CRM systems, but poor setup can frustrate users. Businesses should clearly communicate when a chatbot is in use, ensuring users aren't misled into thinking they're interacting with a human.

- AI phone agents streamline communication. AI-powered phone assistants help businesses manage inbound and outbound calls efficiently, reducing missed opportunities and automating simple inquiries. However, they require continuous updates and refinements to improve accuracy, maintain a positive user experience and avoid misinformation.

Chapter 9

Relationships, Recognition and Revenue

"AI's writing capabilities will certainly improve over time,
but I predict it'll still take longer than you might think to
create something truly great."

Karen Tisdell

Throughout the book-writing process, I've really enjoyed collating insights and musings from fellow real-life humans. (Hopefully, you've enjoyed reading them too.) With my strong emphasis on taking a human-first approach to AI, their inclusion felt essential to me. I didn't want *AI-Human Fusion* to turn into one of the many mundane AI manuals, generic AI-generated guides or prompt-heavy pop-up books that online bookstores are drowning in. I wanted it to feature deeper insights and conversations that aren't typically talked about or are completely overlooked by the "productivity" factor.

While most contributors responded to my "Hear from the humans" callouts with their own human thoughts, there were a few cases of basic AI-generated replies appearing in my inbox. Having a sixth sense for this type of content now, I quickly recognised the responses for what they were and pulled them up on it. While one or two acknowledged the error and re-sent something derived from their own brains, the others seemed to dissolve into the distance.

This habit concerns me because I was very clear that I wanted human insights from human experts for this business book. Maybe they thought quickly produced, AI-generated responses would be good enough and do the job. Maybe they thought I wouldn't notice. Or, maybe they thought it didn't matter. But the truth is, they *weren't* good enough, I *did* notice and it *does* matter. My dream is to push this book out to thousands of professionals across the globe, so reputations are on the line here – both theirs and mine. When it comes to using AI for work, it's important to think about when it's actually helpful and justified versus using it for the sake of it.

You've probably witnessed something similar within your own workplace. Perhaps you've asked a colleague to suggest some ideas for improvement and they've obviously turned to AI to pump something out. Or, you've received an email featuring words you've never heard a team member use in real life. The fact is, as time goes by, more and more people are picking up on the nuances of AI content, so you can't afford to be lazy or let the bots take over.

In this chapter, we look at use cases relating to business-to-business (B2B) interactions where AI can be used effectively to support the humans involved – not replace them.

LinkedIn

Whether you're employed or an entrepreneur, these days we're all feeling increased pressure to create and maintain a strong personal brand on LinkedIn. We're all striving to build that balance of authority and trustworthiness from creating and engaging with organic online content. And we're all determined to build a long line-up of followers. While there are AI tools out there that can help you reproduce the formula of high-engaging posts in your attempt to go viral, I don't recommend taking that path. Otherwise, you fall into the trap of sounding exactly the same as every other person on LinkedIn, fighting the algorithms for a place in your target market's newsfeed.

In addition to not personalising AI-generated social media posts, something that really grinds my gears is when people fall into the trap of using AI to write their comments. When I see AI-generated posts with AI-generated comments, it makes me wonder: what's the point of bots talking to bots? Is this *really* what we want our future to look like? Surely, the aim of these social platforms is to help humans find, connect and collaborate with other humans? We need to be mindful about prioritising productivity and online visibility over what's truly important here.

I know I'm not the only person who feels this way. I asked two knowledgeable LinkedIn coaches, Kate Merryweather and Karen Tisdell, to share some healthy AI habits, highlighting when we should allow AI to enter the LinkedIn stage and when to send it to the back row.

Hear from the humans
Kate Merryweather, LinkedIn Coach

I have tested AI tools for writing LinkedIn posts but haven't been happy with the results. I imagine that's because I haven't given the best instructions. But as I'm building a personal brand on LinkedIn, I think it's really important to inject lots of personality into my posts. I'm also a strong writer and I have spent years honing my skills, so I'm confident that I can write a great post with my brain alone (at this point, because AI is only going to get better and my brain probably is going to slow down!).

But on the other hand, where AI shines is coming up with the ideas for content. I've got some great ideas using AI. Coming up with the content idea is half the battle, so AI tools are excellent for kickstarting that process.

My tips:

- **Do not use AI to comment on posts.** I see plenty of dreary and dull LinkedIn comments that are clearly AI-written. I can see how using AI for commenting is tempting because it's so efficient, but it's not a good look. It's easy for anyone reading to see what's going on. I sometimes visit a person's profile to see their comment history if I suspect the use of AI, and sure enough, there is often a very high volume of posts, all formulaic in nature and all produced at a speed so fast, only the world's best typist would be able to replicate it. I think this lazy approach really damages a person's reputation.

  I recently blocked someone who kept writing "Thanks for the enlightenment, I really learned something" on my posts. It was completely soulless. I asked what she learned, and she never replied, so I felt she was commenting on my content with no intent on having a true conversation with me. So, I blocked her. Getting blocked on LinkedIn is dangerous because if you have too many people blocking you, it can lead to suspension of your account.

- **Inject your own personality.** I'm talking about the type of content that AI isn't great at reproducing. For example, I like to throw in jokes about my love of Barbecue Shapes, Golden Gaytimes, Taylor Swift and 1980s movies. I share funny things my husband and daughters say, and I'm self-deprecating in my humour. This approach helps me show up in a genuine way. So, if anyone meets me in person, they'll feel they already know me quite well. I encourage anyone using AI for LinkedIn to build a personal brand to do the same.

Hear from the humans
Karen Tisdell, LinkedIn Profile Writer

People don't want to look like idiots in front of others, so they don't put themselves out there. But AI has emboldened LinkedIn users to publish a whole lot more content, with more and more people using AI to polish their posts before the world sees them. This means they're one step removed from their own content. So, if something is off about it, well, it isn't their fault. But therein lies the problem.

Yes, AI can cut the waffle and correct your grammar, but it also removes the very human, very relatable messiness that stops us from scrolling. AI doesn't know you. Without proper training, it doesn't know your stories or writing style, your voice or quirky use of grammar. It's likely to struggle to replicate your sense of humour or show your vulnerability. Is this the world we want? The community we crave? Unlikely. Differences make us stronger. Vulnerability and humanity connect us. And LinkedIn is about relationships, so connection is crucial.

My tips:

- **Never use AI to respond to DMs or write invitations to connect.** The AI-generated DM suggestions I've seen are often very salesy. And if too many people report your messages as spam, LinkedIn will suspend your profile. Personalise it with the human touch and run it through the "Mum test". If you write something with AI, think about the approach you'd tell your mum to take if she received a similar message from a random person. Would you advise her to ignore it because it's junk, or respond because it seems legitimate?
- **Don't use AI tools that scrape data from LinkedIn.** Many AI tools and browser extensions claim to scrape (automatically collect) data such as user profiles, posts, connections or emails from LinkedIn. However, LinkedIn explicitly prohibits automated data extraction unless authorised through their official APIs.

Using scraping tools could result in account restrictions, bans or legal action from LinkedIn.

- **Use AI as a metaphor brainstormer.** Metaphors and mini stories light up our brains in a similar way to visual images, making them incredibly effective and engaging for LinkedIn posts. I recommend using your AI tool of choice to animate your content with metaphors, but make it personal. For example, if you love cooking, prompt AI to come up with a clever metaphor that captures your message with imagery related to food.

Award writing

I totally understand that winning business awards is great for enhancing credibility, trust, brand visibility and employee morale. However, if you're thinking of utilising AI to support your award submissions, you need to be careful about your approach. I've been told the gap between the poor- and high-quality entries is widening – and it's usually caused by AI-generated versus human-written content.

While getting my new AI training business off the ground last year, I did some subcontracting as an award writer with Lauren Clemett at The Audacious Agency. Wanting to do the right thing by her business and clients, I nervously asked her if it was okay to use ChatGPT to help me write the award submissions. She was 100% onboard because she knew that I'd take an ethical approach to it all and I had strong copywriting skills to back everything up.

I never asked AI to write the whole submission from start to finish. But I *did* ask it to help transcribe Zoom briefing meetings and draft responses based on the award questions and the client's background information. It came up with some inspiring phrases and ideas, but ultimately it came down to me, as the human, to drive the process. I can proudly say that my efforts led to multiple clients becoming finalists and winning awards.

More recently, I asked Lauren to share her team's current methods when using AI. She says their process begins by fully briefing their Gemini tool about the client by uploading or linking Google Docs and data, case studies, support documents and testimonials – as well as teaching it the client's tone of voice: "You need to give it a full brief, write an overview, and give the AI the context *as well* as the content. The same as if you were briefing a copywriter." (Yes! Thank you!)

Once the brief has been given and entry questions provided, they'll review the draft AI-generated output. However, Lauren advises against copying and pasting this content directly into the award portal: "Use this content as the basis of your entry. Edit and remove typical AI language, check the flow, look for gaps in the information and double-check word count. Read through it expecting AI will get something wrong. Never expect it to be correct!"

While AI is awesome at summarising and storing lots of information, humans still need to step in to connect with the client's story – like knowing what to leave in and what's superfluous. "AI simply doesn't have the ability to create those more subtle or nuanced opportunities to get a message across in a compelling way within a tight word limit while also making it sound personal so the entry stands out from everyone else," adds Lauren.

All-important advice to take onboard next time those award submission deadlines roll around.

Hear from the humans
Lauren Clemett, Founder at The Audacious Agency

We have already heard from awards judges that it is instantly recognisable when an entry is AI-written. Matt Alderton, founder of the Bx Awards and judge of the Telstra Best of Business Awards and Small Business Champion Awards, once told me he can tell an AI-written entry in seconds and that often the prompts are even left in there. Any entry which starts with the phrase "in the fast-paced world of..." or uses verbiage like "fostering", "in conclusion", "in summary" and "we believe" is typical of AI.

There is nothing wrong with using AI to help you write your awards entries but, like everything, judges want to know you've put at least some effort into your entry. It's the same if someone simply pops a press release in as their entry, or doesn't use half the word count available, or fails to add any supporting information. Judges can tell if you are actually invested in the awards process. They care more about that than they do about financial results.

No matter how good AI gets, you still need the human touch for award entries if you want to cut through the competition and get to the finals or even on stage as a winner.

Grants and tenders

While I have limited experience with writing grants and tenders, I'm well aware of the massive scope involved. First, you need to thoroughly understand the evaluation criteria. Then, you need to get onto the research and planning, structuring and writing the submission. After adding the budgeting and financials, you need to review the whole thing and ensure nothing has been missed. And then you cross your fingers and toes and play the waiting game.

As with everything we've talked about in this chapter so far, it would be so much easier to hand it all over to AI to deal with. But you simply can't. I spoke to Melissa Maguire from The Bid Agency for some insights:

> What businesses need to keep in mind is that a compelling and persuasive bid that resonates with the buyer or funder must be solution-focused, outline the features and benefits of your offer,

mitigate risk and be compliant. This is only achievable with human input. Businesses and winning-work champions need to understand that AI-generated responses will only be as good as the human-written prompts. Overall revisions of AI-generated responses are critical in the winning-work process to deliver a compliant, compelling and competitive bid or grant that meets the needs of the buyer or funder.

When asked about her recommended processes for successfully fusing AI and humans, Melissa recommended reading the grant or tender documents fully, highlighting key components and creating bullet points of the features and benefits of your solutions and unique selling propositions (USPs). You also need to jot down notes about how your business will meet the objectives and needs of the buyer or funders. After gaining this clarity, you can bring AI into the picture:

Start by uploading the overall request for tender (RFT) and scope requirements, then creating AI prompts to generate a response to each question. After AI produces a result, you can mould the responses with additional prompts, followed by reviewing and refining further with the human touch in Microsoft Word. I recommend asking AI to generate output using familiar language and keywords in the RFT, scope or grant requirements – plus your brand voice guide if you have one – as this will bring you closer to having a human-centric response in the first draft.

This isn't dissimilar to my article-writing process mentioned earlier. We're just obviously working with a much larger (and weightier) document here.

Hear from the humans
Melissa Maguire CF APMP, Winning Work Champion at
The Bid Agency

AI is amazing at helping us humans save time and structure responses, but only a human can inject the thoughts and emotions into the persuasive and compelling writing needed to influence decision makers.

Put it this way: if your tender or grant first and foremost is compliant and easy to read, then buyers and funders will find it easy to do business with you, and that's a plus from the outset. From there, the decision is based on meeting the needs of the buyer – or, in case of grants, the need in the community. Those needs are human-driven and need to meet the needs of humans, so your grant or tender should be written with the human touch.

Final thoughts...

The overarching lesson from this chapter? Don't rely on cookie-cutter AI output when the reputation and authority of your business is on the line. It might sound amazing at first glance, but it's highly likely to lack "something" – whether that's human emotion or humour, storytelling, correct facts or something else. We need to be the ones driving.

Remember, even driverless cars don't know how to dodge kangaroos at this point!

AI-generated chapter summary *(with human tweaks)*

- AI is reshaping B2B marketing and business operations.
  AI tools are streamlining content creation, LinkedIn
  engagement, award writing and grant submissions, but
  success depends on maintaining a human touch.

- AI-generated LinkedIn content requires caution. While AI can
  help generate ideas and improve efficiency, over-reliance can
  lead to generic posts that lack personality and originality.
  Thought leaders should use AI for ideation but write and
  refine content themselves to build genuine connections.
  Automated comments can be obvious, impersonal and
  even damaging to a professional reputation. Engagement
  on LinkedIn should be human led, ensuring conversations
  remain meaningful.

- AI-assisted award writing improves efficiency. AI can help
  structure responses and generate ideas for business award
  submissions, but judges can easily detect AI-written entries.
  Winning entries require storytelling, emotional appeal and
  careful editing.

- AI supports grant and tender writing. AI can structure
  responses and align language with evaluation criteria, but
  businesses must tailor their applications with a human focus
  on compliance, persuasiveness and buyer needs.

Chapter 10

Bots in the Back Office

"The smartest AI implementation isn't the one that works without humans – it's the one that works brilliantly with them."

Dr Michael G Kollo

In the early days of my AI journey, I went along to a free one-day AI seminar run by a well-known Australian entrepreneur. I totally expected to be sold to throughout the event (which I was), but I also expected to pick up a new learning or two (which I did).

Among all the prompts and tools shared, one thing in particular stood out to me. It was the demonstration of an up-and-coming agentic AI platform. As I mentioned in the glossary at the start of this book, agentic AI involves creating a whole series of agents (aka bots) that are each designed to carry out specific tasks, like a team of virtual assistants – in the true sense of the phrase – working together. These bots don't just perform one job within your company; they all collaborate to complete complex workflows, with the aim of replacing what our human brains would do for certain repetitive or predictable tasks.

During the demonstration, we were shown how bots could pull together content for article creation and repurposing.

Basically, there was a "researcher bot" that sourced relevant information, then passed the process on to a "headline bot" to craft a suitable heading, which then passed it on to a "copywriting bot" to draft the content. A "publishing bot" then took over to upload the article to the website, with a "social media bot" repurposing it all for enhanced exposure. While it scored points in the coolness category, I didn't like that the platform provided the option either to automate completely the process or require manual approvals along the way. By now, you can probably guess which approach I'd prefer – especially as a copywriter. But I imagine most people would just click "automate" and think handing the whole thing over to AI to manage would be a massive time and energy saver.

Handing over internal tasks like this to AI is likely to become a common occurrence in the coming months and years. However, I'd be wary about assuming the technology will do a decent auto-mated job in the early days. As the human "managers", we must bring our experience and expertise to the party – with consideration to possible biases, inaccuracies and ethical concerns.

In this chapter, we dive into use cases for internal workflow and strategic opportunities for AI.

The rise of AI agents

Let's pause for a moment here to consider an important question when it comes to AI agents: what will the future hold if we succumb to these agents and simply allow them to run the whole company for the sake of productivity or cost-cutting? We have a choice here – and we need to make the right one.

We mustn't feel pressured to hand over all creative and critical thinking to AI. Humans still need to manually drive the processes. We still need to be checking they're on track and not running off on their own tangents. And, most importantly, what happens if someone "pulls the plug"? What happens if your company is the victim of a scam, sham, power failure, glitch or some other technical demon – and you've found yourself completely reliant upon these bots? That's when the human brainpower needs to be fired up and act. And hopefully, the expert staff in your organisation haven't been given the sack somewhere along the way as a cost-cutting measure because AI was seen to be an all-knowing power and humans were no longer needed...

To truly understand the power of AI agents, it helps to see where they've come from and how they differ from simple automation processes. Let's have a look at these differences now.

Automation

Automation is the simplest form of task execution. It's all about "if X happens, do Y". Think of it as a digital rule-follower that sticks to a strict playbook, no questions asked. Email filters are a classic use case. For example, you could set it up so that whenever an email arrives with the subject line "Invoice", the system will automatically move it to the "Finance" folder without a second thought. Similarly, if you have booked a meeting via a tool like Calendly, your phone may ping with a notification ten minutes before the scheduled start time.

While incredibly useful for repetitive tasks, automation doesn't adapt or improvise. It works best for predictable scenarios where creativity or decision-making isn't required – just clear, simple instructions.

AI automation

When AI enters the automation scene, it takes things up a notch. It's still about "if X happens, do Y", but it follows a more sophisticated set of steps – with at least one step calling on an LLM for added brainpower. For example, when processing invoices, the system won't just file them away like basic automation would; it can take things a step further by scanning the document, extracting key details like invoice numbers and amounts, and cross-checking them against payment records. When it comes to responding to support tickets, AI automation can be set up to analyse the issue, pull relevant information, draft a helpful response and send it off, all with minimal human input.

It's smarter, more capable and perfect for tasks that require a bit of reasoning – but still follow a predictable flow.

AI agents

Then we have these game-changing bots. Instead of following a fixed set of steps, AI agents are goal-driven – meaning you can ask, "Given goal Y, please figure out the steps (X) to achieve it – and execute them". The magic lies in their ability to adapt and problem-solve along the way. For example, you might ask an AI agent to conduct research on a potential client. It could potentially start by scanning LinkedIn for relevant details, then continue searching for more information if it doesn't find enough on their profile. This may involve pivoting to Google, digging deeper across multiple sources to uncover what it needs.

Every step is part of a flexible, goal-oriented process, with the agent dynamically deciding its next move.

Hear from the humans
Dr Michael G Kollo, CEO at Evolved AI

At the moment, agentic AI or automation is about removing people's existing activities. There's no guarantee that the company will have more work for them to do after those are removed.

However, more technology means better and cheaper products. This ultimately creates demand, creating more jobs – making up for those initially removed tasks.

Mindful implementation of agentic AI

It's key to remember that AI agents are still subject to hallucinations, so we need to keep the expert humans onboard to ensure everything is managed correctly and effectively. As we explore this new territory, setting clear boundaries and keeping that human touch front and centre will ensure AI agents enhance, rather than replace, our expertise.

Here are some questions to consider:

- What specific problems or tasks should AI agents handle?
- How much autonomy should we give them, and where do we set boundaries?
- What data and access will the AI agents require, and how do we protect sensitive information?
- How will we monitor, measure and refine their performance?

AI agents are reshaping workflows, solving problems and freeing us up for bigger, more creative tasks. But their success depends on us. Human oversight, clear boundaries and thoughtful control are absolutely essential.

AI for strategic development

For strategic planning, AI is an incredible partner. The ability to rapidly generate, refine and test ideas means what used to take weeks or months can now be condensed into a much shorter timeframe.

I reached out to Tracy Anthony from Real Minds AI to talk through some of the internal opportunities available to you and your team. She says AI plays two major roles:

1. **Co-creator and brainstorming partner.** AI can challenge assumptions, suggest alternative angles and spark new ideas that mightn't have surfaced in a traditional strategy session. It helps teams break out of habitual thinking patterns,

offering fresh perspectives and encouraging more diverse, creative solutions.

2. **Research tool for deep analysis and iterative prompting.** AI can rapidly sift through data, identifying trends, patterns and insights that might otherwise take weeks to uncover. By layering prompts and refining queries, teams can go beyond surface-level insights, using AI to test different scenarios, validate assumptions and uncover overlooked opportunities.

In the following sections, we touch upon some specific use cases to strategically implement AI across various departments within your company. If you're interested in prompt starters for each area, check out the *AI-Human Fusion* online resources: see the QR code or link provided on page vi.

Hear from the humans
Tracy Anthony, Founder at Real Minds AI

I've been using AI to generate checklists, define project phases and structure workflows. Strategic planning is a cyclical process – you get clear on the direction, then move into implementation. AI helps create structured, executable plans with clear next steps.

Transparency is also key. We openly tell our clients, "We proudly use AI," because it allows us to work more efficiently and deliver better return on investment (ROI). When using AI, I give it clear constraints, like stating that our team consists of just Dennis, myself and AI so it provides recommendations that are actually feasible. When you provide detailed context, the output improves dramatically.

Human resources (HR)

Hiring, onboarding, compliance… yep, your HR team juggles a lot, and the processes aren't getting any simpler. AI can take the heavy lifting out of key tasks, helping businesses find the right candidates faster, streamline paperwork and stay on top of ever-changing regulations. While AI won't replace human judgment in people management, it can free up time for HR teams to focus on what really matters: building a strong, engaged workforce.

AI can streamline HR processes like:

· **Job descriptions and recruitment** – generating position descriptions, matching resumés to job criteria and even creating interview guides
· **Onboarding** – compiling all necessary forms, policies and welcome materials, ensuring new hires get a smooth introduction
· **Payroll and compliance** – cross-checking data with Fair Work Australia and Australian Taxation Office (ATO) regulations, quickly identifying any risks or obligations
· **Performance management** – assisting with setting objectives, aligning KPIs with strategic goals and tracking progress.

However, since HR teams are all about the people, Tracy says we need to remain mindful of privacy: "If you're inputting resumés, you should anonymise personal data. Also, platforms like ChatGPT have privacy settings, so you need to ensure the training mode is switched off so data isn't stored." A good workaround could be using temporary chat features where the conversation disappears once you exit. (Just make sure you save them somewhere safe on your secure platform beforehand.)

Compliance and risk management

I get it, keeping up with regulatory changes can feel like a never-ending game of catch-up, but AI can make it easier to stay ahead and save businesses from last-minute scrambles. Tracy says:

When new legislation is introduced, like critical infrastructure laws or employment reforms, AI can analyse the implications for your business, flag necessary policy updates and even suggest ways to pivot. For example, in one of our webinars we helped National Disability Insurance Scheme (NDIS) businesses adjust their models after major funding changes. AI quickly analysed their services, identified risks, and suggested alternative opportunities they hadn't considered.

I personally know someone who was blindsided by NDIS funding cuts recently. AI could have helped them strategise their next steps to avoid the freak-out.

AI can support compliance and risk management by:

- **updating policies and documentation** – drafting and revising compliance documents to ensure alignment with the latest legal requirements
- **scenario-planning for risk mitigation** – simulating different business scenarios based on potential regulatory changes, helping leaders prepare contingency plans before changes take effect
- **automating compliance checks** – cross-checking company policies against new regulations to highlight gaps and ensure businesses remain compliant without relying solely on legal teams
- **providing industry-specific compliance support** – providing tailored insights based on sector-specific laws and standards, reducing the risk of regulatory oversight
- **protecting against legal risks** – flagging areas where contracts, employee policies or customer agreements may need revision to comply with new regulations, preventing potential legal pitfalls.

Finance and budgeting

While AI can't replace financial experts, it can analyse spending patterns, highlight risks and surface insights that help leaders make smarter financial choices. Instead of drowning in spreadsheets, finance teams can use AI to flag opportunities, reduce risks and ensure contracts are backed by solid data – but always with human oversight.

AI can enhance financial management through:

- **financial insights and forecasting** – analysing historical data to identify spending trends, cash flow risks and potential cost-saving opportunities
- **expense tracking and fraud detection** – flagging unusual transactions and compliance risks, ensuring finance teams can investigate before issues escalate
- **contract and vendor analysis** – reviewing supplier agreements, comparing market benchmarks and highlighting areas where cost optimisations may be possible
- **budget scenario planning** – simulating different financial outcomes to help leaders prepare for best- and worst-case scenarios before making big decisions.

While AI tools can help financial professionals work faster and with greater confidence, every number still needs to be checked and signed off by a qualified expert.

Sales and business development

For those in the hard-working sales teams, AI can help you work smarter by identifying high-potential leads, refining strategies and providing data-driven insights. Instead of wasting time on cold prospects or guesswork, you can focus your energy on building relationships and closing deals.

AI can boost sales through:

- **lead qualification and scoring** – analysing customer data to identify the most promising prospects, allowing sales teams to prioritise their outreach
- **sales pipeline forecasting** – providing insights into deal progression, helping teams anticipate roadblocks and refine their approach
- **personalised outreach** – generating tailored sales emails and proposals based on past interactions and customer preferences
- **competitor and market analysis** – tracking industry trends and competitor activity to uncover new opportunities and stay ahead in the market.

With all this in mind, remember that making sales isn't just about the data – it's about trust, persuasion, and understanding what truly matters to a client. Sure, AI gives sales teams the insights they need to work smarter but, at the end of the day, human relationships still seal the deal.

Final thoughts...

In many ways, this chapter is probably one of the core reasons you picked up this book. While the information isn't exhaustive by any stretch, I wanted to achieve two things here: take on a more humanistic approach to the topic compared to the copy/paste manuals out there, and offer some real-world advice from successful implementations by other businesses and advisors. If you can apply the right balance along with the right strategy, you'll see the fruits of your labour too!

AI-generated chapter summary *(with human tweaks)*

- AI agents are the next evolution of automation. Unlike basic automation, AI agents adapt dynamically to execute tasks, but businesses must set boundaries to prevent over-reliance.

- AI accelerates strategic planning. AI enhances brainstorming and data analysis, but human judgment ensures practical, aligned decision-making.

- AI streamlines HR, compliance, and finance. It optimises hiring, policy updates and financial forecasting, but privacy, accuracy and expert oversight are crucial.

- AI supports sales but can't replace relationships. AI-driven lead scoring and market insights boost efficiency, but trust and human connection remain key to closing deals.

- AI enhances productivity but requires balance. Across all functions, AI is a valuable tool, but human expertise, oversight and strategic implementation are essential for success.

PART III

BUSINESS IMPLEMENTATION

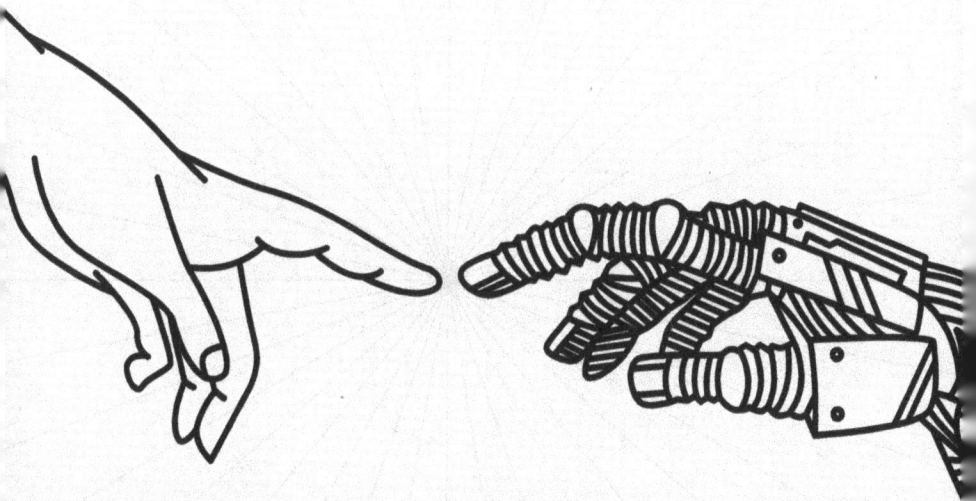

Chapter 11

Ethical and Responsible AI

"Ensuring AI is ethical is a 'human problem' and it's something that can be very subjective. It is challenging to develop objective criteria for ethical AI because everyone thinks differently. We're still trying to define it."

Anmol Agarwal

I was once on an early morning walk with my eldest daughter, who would have been about ten years old at the time. During this beautiful bonding activity, we headed around to the local park, chatting and giggling about various topics. As we walked past the outdoor netball courts, something caught my eye near the silver benches. I did a double take and approached the bench to confirm what I thought I'd seen. Sure enough, there were four folded $20 notes scattered on the concrete beneath the seat.

My first thought? Woah! Eighty bucks – score! But my second thought, which quickly followed, was that pocketing this sum of money wouldn't be ethical. For one, while it wasn't a massive sum by one person's standards, it could be the difference between eating and not eating for the week for another person. I was also extremely conscious that my daughter was watching my every move and wanted to be a good influence. But ultimately, deep down, I knew

I couldn't just take the money without at least attempting to source its owner.

I began by leaving a message with the receptionist at the sports complex that stood within the park's ground. But when I didn't hear back after a week or so, I decided it was best to head to the local police station – and bring both daughters along for the experience. Being a good girl growing up, I'd never set foot in a police station before. I immediately felt like I was guilty of something, even though I was there as a shining Samaritan. My kids seemed equally nervous. But the whole thing went off without a hitch. I explained the situation to the officer and handed over the $80 cash. He wrote down some notes. We then left the station with a spring in our step, knowing we'd taken the most ethical and responsible action.

The outcome? Well, I never received a call from the cops. And I kept forgetting to chase up the station to check in. But then, one day, about two months later, we received a random envelope in the mail addressed to me with the NSW Police logo on the front. My initial reaction was to freak out. What had I done? Accidentally sped through a school zone again? But no. Inside was a cheque for $80. Obviously, no one had claimed the lost cash within a reasonable timeframe, so it was returned to me as the finder.

I could have skipped the whole process and just kept the money in the first place. But my gut knew I had a responsibility to make a genuine effort to locate the original (or more recent) owner of the money. And it felt way more rewarding when the cheque was in my hands.

When it comes to AI, the easy way isn't always the most responsible and ethical way. Unfortunately, time and time again, I'm seeing people focus on the ways AI tools can make their lives easier even if it's to the detriment of others or their company. When you're caught up in the shiny AI hype, sometimes it's hard to

150

see the forest for the trees. However, to avoid the muddy sludge of undesirable AI habits, there are a few key aspects to consider.

While "ethical" and "responsible" are often flung together in the AI space, they refer to different aspects. In this chapter, I dive into both these aspects to help you get a firm grasp on them. I'm thankful to my contributors – Anmol Agarwal, Parul Gupta, Corrie Dark, Mohammed Sabsabi and Dinesh Poorun – for helping me decipher this somewhat ambiguous topic.

Aspects of ethical AI

"Ethical AI" refers to the principles and moral values that guide the development and use of AI systems. It's primarily concerned with what's "right" or "wrong" when designing and deploying AI technologies – always ensuring it's aligned with human values, fairness and rights.

Showing fairness and avoiding bias

AI is only as fair as the data and systems behind it. After all, it comes down to how the humans have trained it. Ensuring fairness means regularly auditing AI models, refining training data and implementing safeguards to prevent discrimination. When left unchecked, AI can reinforce and even amplify existing biases within an organisation, leading to such outcomes as favouring certain demographics in hiring or making unfair decisions in financial approvals. And that's far from ethical.

Parul Gupta, Senior Production Engineer at Meta, says it's important for companies to come up with "fairness constraints" when implementing AI to solve workplace problems or enhance productivity. Rather than looking for the most accurate AI tools in an unrestricted search, she recommends first defining a framework and then finding the best possible solutions within that framework: "Think of it as working within a defined boundary. Rather than searching for the absolute best solution globally, we identify the locally best solution that also meets fairness criteria."

While there are some technical challenges involved when initially training an AI tool, fairness in AI is ultimately a leadership responsibility. Businesses that take the time to define fairness constraints and regularly assess their AI systems can avoid ethical missteps and build technology that genuinely serves their teams, customers and communities.

Here's a sample unethical scenario. Let's say a retail company's CEO introduces an AI-powered hiring tool to streamline recruitment. The AI is trained on past hiring data, which reflects historical biases – favouring certain demographics over others. Rather than auditing or refining the system, leadership prioritises speed and efficiency over fairness, trusting AI to make "data-driven" decisions.

What are the potential repercussions here? To begin with, the company could be slapped with the "discriminatory" label as a result of consistently rejecting candidates from diverse backgrounds due to biased training data. This could then lead to lawsuits for discriminatory hiring practices, resulting in hefty legal fees and financial settlements. If these practices are leaked, customers and partners may boycott the brand, causing long-term revenue loss and a major decline in stock value. Worst-case scenario: the backlash forces the CEO to step down, causing the company irreversible reputational damage and potentially leading to bankruptcy.

❛ Hear from the humans
Parul Gupta, Senior Production Engineer at Meta

Fairness in AI is fundamentally about reducing bias, but it's not as straightforward as drawing a strict line between biased and

I'm setting an ethical example of how humans should work with accessible technology.

Even though I'm (obviously) writing a book about AI, I've been extremely mindful about falling into the trap of just asking ChatGPT to write this book for me. This is partly because I've seen the countless, poorly AI-written-books about AI flooding online bookstores and partly because various people cheekily asked me in the early stages, "So, are you just going to get AI to write it?" I knew *AI-Human Fusion* had to be different. I had to practise what I preach. And since I'm a writer by trade, I knew I'd be extremely hypocritical (and somewhat embarrassed) if I handed over the writing process to the bots.

However, I'm not a complete idiot. Since I know how to collaborate with the ChatGPT buddy from a human-centred perspective, it would have been silly of me to ignore it completely. Every time I have been stuck and sought assistance for chapter structure, interview questions, conclusions or definitions, I've kept tabs on the prompts and dumped them into a document. In the *AI-Human Fusion* online resources you can find every single prompt and output used at every stage of writing: see the QR code or link provided on page vi.

To me, this is a perfect example of transparency. (And I hope I inspire others to do the same!) But let's look at a non-transparent scenario. Say a health insurance company introduces an AI-powered chatbot to handle policyholder inquiries, claims and complaints. Instead of ensuring transparency, leadership intentionally hides the fact that customers are interacting with AI, making the bot sound human while avoiding proper escalation to real agents. The chatbot is also programmed to delay claim approvals and subtly mislead customers about their coverage, reducing payouts and increasing profits. The potential consequences could range from customer dissatisfaction, leading to consumer protection agencies investigating the company for deceptive practices, to class-action lawsuits, to possible bankruptcy. So, yes, completely ordinary customer interactions could potentially lead to extraordinary (and damaging) outcomes.

Accountability and integrity

AI may be built on data and algorithms, but the responsibility for its decisions always falls on the humans who create and deploy it. Ethical AI involves designing systems that function well and ensuring they operate fairly, transparently, and without harm. Companies must take ownership of how AI is trained, what biases it might inherit, and the real-world impact of its outputs. For example, if an AI system discriminates in hiring, spreads misinformation or makes decisions that negatively affect people, you can't just blame the technology. Someone in leadership or an expert in the area needs to step in, take corrective action, and ensure your AI is working for your employees and customers, not against them.

Over the last couple of years, I've noticed the lines are often blurred between the terms "Generative AI" and "automation". Many people think they're the same thing, but they're actually not. However, one does follow the other. Think of it this way: GenAI produces unique content based on patterns in data, while automation streamlines repetitive tasks using predefined rules. So, step one involves creating your strategies and content with GenAI, and step two involves setting up the automation systems. For example, I drafted an email sequence in collaboration with ChatGPT, then uploaded the emails to the "Automations" section in Mailchimp, setting them up to be automatically sent one by one to anyone who downloads a copy of "Your AI-Humanisation Checklist". (By the way, this is available to you via the *AI-Human Fusion* online resources: see the QR code or link provided on page vi.)

The most ethical consideration when it comes to automation is to automate with intention. You want to ensure every AI-driven process serves a real purpose, supports human decision-making and ultimately benefits both your business and the people it impacts. Because no matter how advanced AI becomes, strategy, empathy and accountability will always be human jobs.

Corrie Dark, Technology Advisor at Integrity AI, agrees with me:

> *Automation must be secondary to human decision-making and ongoing oversight and assessment. Like any other tool, AI technology is not magical and omniscient. It needs constant refinement as we uncover oversights in the initial brief and find new opportunities for it to solve.*
>
> *Technology is also literal. We give it a specific problem and it will work to solve only that problem. Humans, on the other hand, have a unique ability to see more broadly. We can identify gaps and additions that will make the AI technology solution better. The role of humans is to continually test and assess the definition of "complete" to ensure AI functions properly.*

We always need to think about the needs of our customers and business first. It's easy to get swept up in the AI hype, assuming the technology will magically solve inefficiencies or offer new levels of productivity. But without careful oversight, it can just as easily create more problems, like misaligned messaging, impersonal customer experiences or even ethical breaches. This is why I encourage you to keep the humans involved when it comes to assessing and dealing with customer reviews, feedback and complaints. I know of many companies that already have awful dispute resolution processes, and just throwing AI bots into the mix to handle the issues may cause further harm.

True ethical AI also requires integrity – you know, the commitment to doing what's right, even when it's inconvenient. Just because AI can generate content faster, personalise marketing at scale or optimise processes doesn't mean it should be used without a second thought. As already mentioned, transparency is key, and businesses should be upfront about when and how AI is influencing decisions. You need to prioritise fairness over speed, accuracy over convenience and trust over unchecked automation. It's about using AI to create a positive impact, not just to streamline processes.

Hear from the humans
Corrie Dark, Technology Advisor at Integrity AI

The main thing is to get involved. It doesn't matter whether you're in a leadership position, on a company board, or you're a human being using modern technologies in your day-to-day life. It's critical that you understand what you're using and what's underneath it.

The challenge with even simple AI technologies like LLMs or GenAI is that we only see the tip of the iceberg when we're using it. By that I mean when we use ChatGPT, we don't see what's going on underneath – where it's getting the information from, how reliable its sources are, and how the commercial imperatives of the company that owns the AI model might impact the answers provided. ChatGPT is not a qualified research assistant. It's an eager-to-please toddler running around finding information that matches your question.

Privacy and data protection

AI systems thrive on large amounts of information, but that doesn't mean businesses can be careless with how they collect, store, or use it. Privacy includes both internal compliance as well as respecting your customers, employees, and stakeholders by ensuring their data isn't exploited or mishandled. Without proper safeguards, AI can easily become intrusive rather than innovative.

Since one of the biggest ethical responsibilities in AI is handling data with care, I felt it was important to do a proper deep dive into this topic in Chapter 13: AI Security without the Stress. We will explore this area more shortly.

Yes, there's a lot to unpack when it comes to ethical AI. For those based in Australia, you can find out more by reading Australia's AI Ethics Principles online. Another document to review is the Australian Government's Voluntary AI Safety Standard. Initially released in September 2024, it aims to help organisations develop and implement AI systems in our country through 10 voluntary guardrails. I've had the honour of being involved in a roundtable discussion via the National AI Centre to help determine the next steps forward. I'm interested to see where things go from here. If you're based overseas, check out your government websites for information relevant to your own backyard.

Aspects of responsible AI

While "ethical AI" refers to the principles governing the use of AI, "responsible AI" is a practical and operational approach to implementing those principles. Basically, it transforms ethical principles into actionable policies and governance to prevent issues.

Risk management

While AI brings new opportunities, it also introduces a bunch of risks – some we've covered and some we explore in the next two chapters. As a leader, you have the challenge of adopting AI as well as ensuring it's implemented safely, ethically, and in alignment with broader organisational risk frameworks. While the world of AI is new for most, there's not a lot of space for hesitation or procrastination here. If you haven't already, you need to be prepared to address the risks involved.

The reality is, AI risk mitigation follows the same principles as any other business risk: proactive planning, informed decision-making and ongoing oversight. Mohammed Sabsabi, co-founder of Rapid AI 4 Learning, says:

> *The first step to overcome these challenges and show leadership is to understand that mitigating AI risks requires the same values and processes to mitigate any other organisational risk, such as work health and safety, compliance, cybersecurity, finance, and so on. AI mitigation is a conglomeration of safety, risk, compliance and governance all rolled into one.*
>
> *The second step is for leaders to start now and be a star later. Leaders can do this by forming networks, even with competitors, as they do when negotiating pay awards and industry standards. The initial design and implementation will not be perfect, but the absence of mitigation processes and strategies is a much more high-risk alternative.*

In summary, you're better off taking some form of informed action now. The longer businesses delay, the greater the risk of falling behind or making reactive, high-stakes decisions later. If you're one of the leaders taking a proactive approach, collaborating with industry peers and embedding risk strategies into your existing governance frameworks, you'll be in one of the best positions for long-term success.

Hear from the humans
Anmol Agarwal, Senior Security Researcher at Nokia and Founder at Alora Tech LLC

Leaders should evaluate whether they truly will benefit from using an AI solution, because sometimes AI is just too computationally expensive to justify being used. If there's a simpler approach that gives the company the same results with a similar performance, that should be used over AI. Leaders should do a cost-benefit analysis before using AI as well.

In addition, leaders should have diverse teams with different people from different fields so that the organisation can collaboratively determine AI strategies. This means having subject-matter experts like AI researchers and data scientists as well as leaders and developers on the team.

Leaders should also prioritise designing AI with security in mind and, whenever possible, use explainable AI to explain how AI arrived at its decisions. If the AI tool gives a result, a team of people should verify and check it prior to taking any action. AI can make mistakes, so being able to explain how AI came up with a decision and having a safeguard in place in the event of a wrong decision is very important.

Sustainability and social impact

AI has the potential to drive sustainability efforts, from optimising energy use to improving climate modelling and supply-chain efficiency. But the technology itself actually comes with a cost. AI models require massive computational power, leading to high energy consumption and environmental impact. Personally, I believe this area of AI isn't talked about enough in day-to-day conversations – especially when sustainability has been on the global agenda for decades. So, I've done a bit of research for you.

More than 190 countries have adopted a series of non-binding recommendations on the ethical use of AI, which covers the environmental impact. Both the European Union and the United States of America have introduced legislation, but policies like those are few and far between. Golestan (Sally) Radwan, Chief

Digital Officer of the United Nations Environment Programme (UNEP), says:

> *There is still much we don't know about the environmental impact of AI, but some of the data we do have is concerning. We need to make sure the net effect of AI on the planet is positive before we deploy the technology at scale ... Governments are racing to develop national AI strategies, but rarely do they take the environment and sustainability into account. The lack of environmental guardrails is no less dangerous than the lack of other AI-related safeguards.*

So, what are the environmental issues at play? Well, most large-scale AI systems run in data centres, which are huge facilities powered by cloud service providers. But while AI might feel like an invisible force, its environmental footprint is definitely making an imprint. These data centres demand vast amounts of raw materials, with 800 kg of resources required to produce a single 2 kg computer. The microchips that drive AI models rely on rare earth elements, which are often mined in ways that cause significant environmental harm.

Then there's the issue of electronic waste. AI hardware doesn't last forever, and when discarded it can release hazardous substances like mercury and lead into the environment. On top of that, data centres require huge amounts of water, both during construction and for ongoing cooling. According to the report *Making AI Less "Thirsty": Uncovering and Addressing the Secret Water Footprint of AI Models*, AI-related infrastructure could soon consume six times more water than Denmark, at a time when one in four people worldwide already struggle to access clean water.

And of course, powering AI's complex systems takes a massive amount of energy. In many places, that is still provided by burning fossil fuels, driving up carbon emissions. A single ChatGPT request uses 10 times more electricity than a Google search. With the number of data centres surging from 500,000 in 2012 to over 8 million today, AI's demands on the planet are only growing.

While big-picture solutions are currently being investigated, we can still play a role in overcoming the sustainability challenge. According to the recent EY research paper *AI and Sustainability: Opportunities, Challenges, and Impact*, there are four key areas of focus:

1. **Computing power.** The more complex an AI model, the more processing power it demands. AI systems run millions of calculations behind the scenes, so the heavier the workload, the greater the strain on global infrastructure.
2. **Energy consumption.** Cloud providers track energy usage, but many AI systems still rely on fossil-fuel-powered data centres, increasing carbon emissions.
3. **Carbon footprint.** Apart from how much energy is used, AI's environmental cost is also about where that energy comes from. Businesses need to consider how data centres are powered, with some using metrics like carbon usage effectiveness (CUE) to measure impact. However, hidden emissions from supply chains and infrastructure make this a complex issue.
4. **Water usage.** Cooling AI hardware requires enormous amounts of water. Some estimates predict AI-related infrastructure could soon consume more water than entire countries. Metrics like water usage effectiveness (WUE) can help track usage, but businesses need to be aware of AI's growing strain on global water resources.

As businesses continue to integrate AI, its environmental footprint can't be ignored. While AI has the potential to support sustainability efforts, it also contributes to resource depletion, carbon emissions and water consumption. The key isn't to abandon AI but to be smarter about how we use it – tracking energy usage, optimising computing power and pushing for more sustainable practices. AI should be part of the solution, not another contributor to an ongoing global problem.

Hear from the humans
Mohammed Sabsabi and Dinesh Poorun, Co-founders at Rapid AI 4 Learning

Sustainability is a very important ethical consideration when considering the cost of AI and our over-reliance on chatbots, LLMs and "chip" processing. To keep the machines learning, there's a cost to the finite resources of the planet. Some modelling shows every ChatGPT query is like a bottle of water in terms of resource usage. Water and electricity usage is surging to meet the global demands of using LLMs and bots like ChatGPT. Businesses, governments, industries and AI summits like the AI Action Summit in Paris in 2025 need to embed sustainable development into AI policies and legislation. AI environmental impact needs to be included in countries' carbon emissions targets as well.

There is also a question to consider for future generations: if we are over-reliant on AI today, and the resources we are using are finite, what will the quality of life be like for future generations? Will there need to be AI restrictions in the same way that we have water restrictions now? How will that impact a world that is becoming more reliant on this technology?

Governance and compliance

AI doesn't eliminate responsibility. In fact, it demands more of it. Businesses can't shrug off poor outcomes by blaming "the algorithm", or assume AI will always get it right. Every AI-driven decision should be traceable, with clear oversight of who is responsible for its development, deployment and impact. This means setting up governance frameworks, regularly auditing AI systems and ensuring that when something goes wrong, humans – not machines – step in to fix it.

This is why establishing an AI policy is absolutely key for your organisation. Before your team runs wild with AI tools, you need clear rules. What's allowed? Where are the restrictions? Who owns the AI-generated content? And how do you stay compliant while still keeping up with the digital world? I'll be covering this topic and more in Chapter 12: Protect Your Business, Protect Your IP.

Final thoughts...

Ethical and responsible AI is partly about following rules and partly about making deliberate, human-centred choices. AI may optimise processes, but it also carries real-world consequences, from bias and misinformation to sustainability concerns.

Leaders must take ownership of how AI is used, ensuring it aligns with fairness, transparency and accountability. In the rush to adopt new tools, the easiest option isn't always the right one. So, take a moment (but not too many) to consider how your company can use AI ethically, responsibly and with integrity.

AI-generated chapter summary *(with human tweaks)*

· Ethical AI focuses on fairness, transparency and human values, while Responsible AI ensures these principles are actively implemented through governance and risk management.

· AI models can reinforce biases if not carefully managed. Businesses must establish fairness constraints, regularly audit their AI systems and ensure decisions are inclusive and equitable.

- Transparency matters, so AI-generated content should be clearly labelled to maintain trust and prevent misinformation. Being open about AI's role in business decisions helps customers and employees make informed choices.

- Leaders must be accountable and lead with integrity. They must take ownership of AI-driven outcomes, ensuring technology is used ethically and that human oversight remains a priority.

- AI introduces new risks, including bias, security threats and regulatory challenges. Proactive planning, ongoing monitoring and industry collaboration help businesses mitigate these risks effectively.

- AI infrastructure consumes significant energy, water and raw materials, contributing to global sustainability concerns. Businesses must consider AI's resource demands and adopt strategies to reduce its footprint.

- AI should be embedded into existing risk and compliance frameworks. Establishing clear AI policies ensures alignment with industry regulations and ethical standards.

Chapter 12

Protect Your Business, Protect Your IP

"Artificial intelligence isn't just creating new works,
it's challenging the concept of authorship, ownership,
and originality in intellectual property law."

Michelle Gorton

Back in January 2024, I received a LinkedIn message out of the blue from a woman I'd shared a stage with two years before. She reached out to say she'd been following my successful business pivot and had started "delving into the AI space" herself – but as an intellectual property (IP) lawyer. Over the prior 12 months, she'd been presenting talks about AI and the effects on IP – and suggested possible collaboration opportunities.

I'm not sure what the visual equivalent is for ears pricking up, but that's what my eyes did when I read Michelle Gorton's message. (Eyes popped out of my head? Hmm, not sure.) I knew I wasn't, and could never be, across every aspect of AI, especially when it came to the legal side of things. I. Was. Not. Touching. That.

So, we grabbed a coffee together, and a lovely business relationship began to flourish. Michelle popped into my Meetup group one time as a guest presenter in mid-2024, and in early 2025 we co-hosted a masterclass. At the time of writing, we've just kicked off a collaboration on an AI policy offering for organisations via her legal firm, Gorton IP.

I also invited her to play a large role in this chapter by co-writing it with me. Oh, how I love collaborations. Thanks, Michelle!

When it comes to IP in the ever-growing world of artificial intelligence, you simply can't afford to bury your head in the sand. Because as AI continues to revolutionise industries everywhere, it's becoming more and more essential for organisations and individuals to learn how to navigate the complexities of IP laws to protect innovations and avoid potential disputes.

Please note: this chapter covers IP issues related to AI in Australia and globally, based on laws in place at the time this book was published.

What is IP in AI?

In general, "intellectual property" (IP) refers to the legal rights that protect creations of the mind, including but not limited to inventions, literary and artistic works, designs, symbols and brand names. When looking at AI, there are a few ways that IP gets involved.

AI-generated content

AI-generated content is content created by AI systems, which includes, but is not limited to, text, music, videos, visual art and code. The legal status of this type of content is complex, because traditional copyright laws generally require human authorship. (Hmm, interesting times ahead as the legal world catches up...) Right now, questions are frequently popping up around whether AI-generated works can be protected by copyright and, if they can, who owns the rights: the AI developer, the user, or no one at all?

Under current copyright laws in most jurisdictions, including Australia and overseas, copyright protection still requires a human author. Therefore, without original human input, AI-generated content will most likely not qualify for copyright protection. It's interesting to note some countries are considering new legal frameworks surrounding this issue, while others remain firm that human input is of prime importance.

I'd like to share a personal story here. A friend of mine recently started a new business and enthusiastically forwarded me her logo "hot off the press!". It only took a quick glance for me to recognise it as AI-generated. The logo looked extremely similar to those produced by my Malaysian students as part of their mock company projects in their two-day AI workshops – logos that had been produced with Dall-E 3 via ChatGPT. Something about the design style and font jumped out at me. Out of concern, I (carefully) asked her whether it had been created with AI.

It turns out she'd used a graphic designer friend to do the design, who – after some questioning from my side – later admitted to using AI and making changes via Illustrator. From my experience with AI-generated images to date, they can't seem to spell very well, even if you have spelled everything correctly in your prompt. So, I have a sneaking suspicion the wording was the only thing that was changed. Because when I popped onto ChatGPT myself, I found it was super easy to create a *very* similar logo, using similar colours and font, with only a very basic one- or two-line prompt (aka briefing).

While she won't get in trouble for using this AI-generated logo, the problem is that someone else may generate, download and use an identical or similar logo to her. It's something to be mindful of – especially if you're investing in a designer to produce original work.

AI algorithms and models

There are lots of technologies out there being produced by intelligent, tech-savvy humans, such as machine learning models, neural networks and AI-powered software applications, which all represent valuable IP. These are typically protected under patents, copyright, designs or trade secret laws, depending on the nature of the innovation.

However, the patent eligibility of AI-related inventions remains a controversial issue. Not only does it come down to the extent of these AI-generated models and algorithms meeting the requirements of novelty and inventiveness, they face additional fundamental patentability requirements in many jurisdictions. For example, in Australia, generally the algorithms must improve the performance of a computer (or network) or result in a technical effect outside the computer.

Training data

AI systems rely on massive amounts of data to learn and improve. If you're using "off-the-shelf" AI tools like ChatGPT, Copilot or Gemini, this data may include a mix of publicly available information and copyrighted materials. There are a fair few legal battles currently taking place around the world due to AI models being trained on protected works without explicit authorisation.

Questions relating to data ownership, licensing, privacy rights and potential copyright infringement are big issues right now. Only time will tell how it will all unfold.

For those with the funds, I recommend building your very own GenAI tool that is purely trained on your organisation's data and content – without being infiltrated with any external, possibly unethically sourced sources. While this is the best practice to avoid tapping into copyright issues, it's unfortunately financially inaccessible for smaller businesses at this stage. (In other words, you need the big bucks!)

AI-assisted innovations

With AI presenting exciting opportunities due to its capability to come up with new ideas and use "advanced reasoning", it's starting to play a crucial role in developing new inventions. As a result, it's raising questions about whether AI can be recognised as an inventor or co-inventor of a patent.

Current patent systems generally require human inventorship, so AI has thrown a major spanner in the works. There are currently ongoing legal debates and policy discussions to address how AI-assisted innovations should be treated under patent law, particularly in cases when AI contributes significantly to the inventive step.

What's an inventive step, you ask? Well, it's the process of coming up with a new and inventive idea. The idea must be novel, involve an inventive step and be industrially applicable in order for it to have a chance to be a patentable invention. To what extent was the human involved? Did they come up with the original idea, or was it generated by AI? Was all the research conducted by humans, with the data collated fed to the tools for the next step? Or, were humans barely part of the process at all?

There's an Australian case law that tested whether AI can be listed as an inventor. As at the date of the publication of this book, AI cannot be recognised as an inventor under Australian law, as the *Patents Act 1990* (Cth) requires an inventor to be a natural person.

How AI and IP should play together

Michelle has kindly pulled together some helpful recommendations of ways to safeguard your ownership of AI-generated content:

- **Branding and logos.** Protect any AI-related branding and logos by registering a trademark. Please note, if you're using any AI programs to generate the trademark, ensure you read the terms and conditions of the program to determine who's the owner of the name or logo, as well as the usage rights.

- **Copyright protection.** Add strong human input to any AI-generated content for legal protection. For example, AI-generated logos may lack the human authorship required for copyright protection, which may affect the enforcement of your IP rights.
- **Patents.** You can file patents for AI-related innovations, including software applications and algorithms, if they solve a technical problem in a novel way. However, in most countries an AI system can't be listed as an inventor. Only a human who contributed to the invention can claim authorship. If an invention is fully AI-generated, obtaining a patent is unlikely in Australia.
- **Confidentiality and security.** To safeguard your trade secrets, keep your AI models, datasets and processes confidential through non-disclosure agreements and restricted security access.
- **IP ownership.** Clearly define IP ownership and rights in contracts when collaborating with developers, AI service providers or third-party vendors.

Hear from the humans
Michelle Gorton, Managing Partner at Gorton IP

Ensuring originality is the key here.

To avoid IP disputes, aim to use AI tools that don't infringe on copyrighted materials. Don't train your AI models on copyrighted materials without licence or authorisation. This is very important. You also need to avoid publishing AI-generated content that replicates existing works. As a tip, I recommend obtaining plagiarism detection software to check AI-generated content before publication and to add your own original thoughts and ideas to the work. It's a good idea to keep records of human involvement in AI-assisted creation to establish copyright eligibility down the track as well.

If unsure, consult a legal professional to ensure your AI usage aligns with the laws in Australia or overseas.

What is an AI policy, and why do we need one?

If you haven't already, you're likely to start hearing about AI policies everywhere. In our opinion, they'll soon become an essential piece in AI regulation.

An AI policy is a document that outlines guidelines, principles and procedures for the development and use of AI within an organisation or jurisdiction. The aim is to ensure AI technologies are being utilised ethically, responsibly and in compliance with relevant laws and regulations in the relevant country. It's an official document that helps ensure a balance between innovation and transparency, both internally and externally to your company, in an AI-infused world.

Why do you need an AI policy? To put it simply, it could help you protect yourself and your company in the future. We believe every business, from large companies to startups, needs to make obtaining an AI policy a priority.

Here's a quick run-down on what an effective AI policy should include:

- **IP ownership and licensing.** How do you define IP ownership for AI-generated works?
- **Copyright compliance.** What are your procedures for monitoring AI-generated content to prevent copyright infringement?
- **Rules surrounding the use of AI-generated content.** When is AI usage permissible, and when must it be avoided?

- **Security measures for handling proprietary training data.**
  How are you protecting trade secrets? What type of data is
  safe to upload or share with AI tools for training purposes?
- **Guidelines to prevent AI misuse and biases.** How will you
  ensure ethical, trustworthy and transparent usage within
  your organisation?
- **Any legal considerations.** What potential issues could arise,
  both internal and external, from the implementation of AI?

If you're lacking clarity in these areas, with no official documentation, you're asking for trouble. Especially if you have countless people within your organisation using AI without proper education and awareness of the consequences of unethical, non-compliant or unsecure practices. While there is a range of publicly available AI policies online to view as examples, we recommend consulting a legal professional to develop an AI policy tailored to your organisation.

Final thoughts...

While the rules are still evolving in this space, one thing is clear: businesses and creators need to be proactive. That means understanding the basics of IP, protecting original work, avoiding copyright headaches and putting smart AI policies in place. As laws catch up with technology, staying informed and getting solid legal advice will help you stay on the right side of compliance while keeping your ideas safe.

Watch this space.

AI-generated chapter summary *(with human tweaks)*

- AI is shaking up intellectual property (IP). Traditional ideas of authorship, ownership and originality are being questioned as AI generates creative works.

- Copyright laws require human authorship. AI-generated content, from text to logos, often lacks legal protection because it isn't created by a natural person.

- AI-generated logos pose a risk. Designs can be easily replicated by others, raising concerns about originality and brand protection.

- AI-created innovations struggle to qualify for patents, as most laws require a human inventor.

- AI training data raises legal questions. AI models rely on large amounts of data, often including copyrighted material, leading to lawsuits and ethical concerns.

- Can AI be a co-inventor? Legal systems say no (for now), but debates continue.

- Protecting AI-generated work – best practices include:
  - registering trademarks for branding and logos
  - ensuring strong human input in AI-generated content for copyright protection
  - filing patents for AI-related innovations if they meet legal criteria
  - using NDAs and security measures to protect proprietary AI models and data
  - clearly defining IP ownership in contracts with developers and vendors.

- AI policies are becoming essential – businesses need clear guidelines on:
  - who owns AI-generated content
  - how to handle copyright compliance and licensing
  - when AI-generated content is acceptable (or not)
  - security measures for proprietary data
  - preventing AI misuse and bias.

Chapter 13

AI Security Without the Stress

"With AI, there's a risk of private information being leaked to other users. Some argue it's not the actual data being leaked but a transformation of it. Still, that creates anxiety – what if sensitive information unintentionally gets out?"

Terence Kam

Just like IP, my understanding of AI security is fairly basic. But I'm extremely aware I need to be mindful when it comes to providing advice and information to my followers and students. The last thing I want is to unintentionally get anyone in trouble – or, even worse, sued!

Usually, I train teams and entrepreneurs about how to use GenAI for basic day-to-day tasks. And when it comes to entering data into those GenAI tools, I say if the content is something you'd share on your website or happily send to a client, it's fine to upload. On the other hand, if it contains information that would result in your worst nightmare if it escaped to the outside world, it's probably best to keep it away from the bots.

I recently crossed paths with a potential training client who runs a small legal firm – where security is absolutely paramount. Through our lengthy in-person conversation, I explained all the untapped opportunities of utilising a GenAI tool for his team. It couldn't just improve their email communications; it could also provide much-appreciated time-saving support for dealing with court cases. I enthusiastically explained how amazing it would be if his team could train their tool to completely understand a full case by accessing all the relevant paperwork, then provide insights about the judge allocated to the case and ask AI to provide suggestions of possible biases or objections. Then they could be completely prepared for court, minus the long hours at the office and sleepless nights. Obviously, he was on board with that idea. He also appreciated my human-centric approach and was keen to conduct team training with me.

While we were both eager to get started, I was completely transparent about my security and privacy concerns. I said that while Copilot would seem the obvious choice with their Microsoft software integration, meaning it could access their documents on SharePoint, I had recently become aware of the *USA PATRIOT Act*, which many of the big players in the GenAI space are held to. This act was passed after 9/11 to help the US government track down and stop potential terrorist threats. It gave authorities more power to monitor phone calls, emails and financial transactions – but also sparked debates about privacy. Some parts of the law have since changed or expired as the government tries to balance security with personal freedom. With AI posing lots of potential security issues, there are definitely risks around having your data released if there is any sense of uncertainty.

After uncovering these details about the *USA PATRIOT Act*, from an ethical and security point of view I just couldn't assure him and his team that sensitive client information would remain 100%

protected. I then started the hunt for more secure, Australian-based GenAI tools that I could trust – platforms that were outside US jurisdiction. At the time of writing, I'm still researching those platforms, because I want to protect both myself and my clients.

So, what happened with my legal client? Well, I've kept him in the loop about the few platform providers I'm speaking with. I reached out to him recently to check whether he'd prefer to proceed with basic training on Copilot, excluding tasks that involve sensitive data, or wait until I source a secure solution. He was completely supportive and appreciative of my transparency and updates, and said he's willing to wait. I'm well aware that not all AI trainers would be as ethical as I am – they'd jump into the training without a second thought. I don't operate like that.

In this chapter, I walk you through the biggest security and privacy issues you need to be aware of to protect yourself, your team and your organisation. I've sought insights from two cybersecurity consultants: Terence Kam, author of *Easy Guide to Cybersecurity & Privacy* and founder of iSecurityGuru, and Nakshathra Suresh, cyber criminologist and co-founder at eiris. I've known Terence for many years via the networking circuit and was lucky enough to e-meet Nakshathra at an online roundtable discussion for the National AI Centre. I'm very grateful to both experts for co-writing this chapter with me. Thanks, guys!

Why we need to be wary about AI security and privacy

I've personally heard about various large Australian companies that were extremely hesitant to introduce GenAI to their work practices due to the potential security and privacy risks involved. Staff were initially forbidden from using this new accessible technology until they worked out what they were truly dealing with. As I type these words, it's been two and a half years since the release of ChatGPT, and things are slowly changing. Many companies are investing in secure, private platforms or telling staff to proceed with caution and avoid sharing sensitive information. I'm also hearing about the murky waters involved when it comes to AI bot note-takers appearing in corporate Google Meet and Zoom meetings – with or without an accompanying human. This sparks privacy concerns, because it's not always clear who is "listening in", and there's the potential for meeting transcripts to be misused. Something said "off the record" could wind up being used against someone, or a transcript could be easily passed on to a colleague who shouldn't be privy to the content of the discussion. So, that's something you need to be wary of too.

Returning to GenAI tools, they simply can't effectively serve humans without being trained on massive amounts of data – and that may possibly include a mix of personal, sensitive and proprietary information. While we don't have proof that this is happening, many of us have strong suspicions. These suspicions are fuelled by leaked corporate practices. like Facebook's privacy policy indicating they train their model on users' public posts. There were also recent allegations that Mark Zuckerberg approved Meta's use of "pirated" versions of copyright-protected books for AI training purposes.

If not properly secured, the users' data input (aka what we tell or ask the tool to do) could be exposed through cyberattacks, data breaches or unintended leaks.

While some tools provide you with a privacy settings toggle, enabling you to choose whether it's okay for them to use your data to train the models, we still can't know for sure how our data is being stored, processed or shared. Some vague details are usually featured in the tool privacy policies, and in some instances it's easy to see the red flags. But other times, the legal speak makes it a little harder to uncover what's actually happening with our data.

On top of it all, the rise of AI-generated content presents unsavoury opportunities for creating deep fakes, misinformation and identity theft. This is one of the core reasons why I'm not actively creating digital avatars of myself or training bots on how to speak in my voice. Being a public figure and being featured on countless podcasts and YouTube videos, it's already possible for someone to maliciously attempt to replicate me. I don't need to make things even easier for them by getting caught up in the shiny "coolness" factor.

As AI becomes more embedded in daily life, we must all take responsibility by staying informed about privacy settings, data policies and the potential risks of relying too heavily on automated systems. You might have an IT team to guide you, but it's up to you as a leader to ensure best practices are being carried out by you and your team.

Hear from the humans
Nakshathra Suresh, Cyber Criminologist and Co-founder at eiris

For me, AI literacy is key. I have attended so many public speaking engagements where individuals at companies have not been provided with the necessary training, education or resources to understand the merits and the disadvantages of using Generative AI.

Proactive steps you can take are to access actual evidence-based research courses and short-form training, as well as bringing in expert AI trainers to explain how to use these platforms in your day-to-day life. Because a lot of the time I feel like organisations are trying to keep AI hidden. It's almost like, "out of sight, out of mind". They seemingly don't really care if their employees are using ChatGPT to inform their work, but they also don't really know about the harms that result.

Establishing a secure AI environment

Terence advises there's a fundamental cybersecurity issue with GenAI tools, because one of the basic principles in cybersecurity is never to mix data and commands together in the same pipeline. Tools like ChatGPT and Copilot ignore that principle, pulling both data and commands together with no segregation. The leaking of sensitive information is just one possible consequence of this vulnerability, which is technically called a "prompt injection attack". It basically involves an attacker creating a prompt that tricks the model into doing something it shouldn't, like tricking the tools to reveal how to write malware code or make a bomb.

In most cases, the only way for GenAI companies (like Microsoft and OpenAI) to deal with these attacks is to respond reactively. Terence says:

> Hackers will find a security hole, then the company will patch it up. Then hackers will find another, and the cycle repeats. It's always a cat-and-mouse game. This is inevitable because the fundamental cybersecurity principle is being violated. There's been a massive amount of effort at the hardware, software and processing levels to keep data and commands separate. But the problem with ChatGPT (and similar) is that it keeps mixing the two back together.

The security risks are even higher when AI is given the power to make decisions. For example, an airline chatbot could be tricked into altering the price of an airline ticket to $1. To stop these types of complications from occurring, humans must always be involved in your AI processes. For example, Terence recently wanted to close a bank account, so he collaborated with his bank's chatbot to gather helpful information about the process. Thankfully, the chatbot wasn't given the power to close the bank account itself, but it had been trained to pass the client on to a human team member to action the request. The chat transcript then provided useful background details to speed up the process.

So, what can we do to protect ourselves? Companies can seek private versions of GenAI that are segregated from public systems and built specifically for company use. All data, training and operations stay confined to the organisation. But, of course, it comes with a cost. So, if you don't have the funds, it's just a matter of being wary about your habits.

Taking an "offline" approach is another idea being investigated. It involves running AI models on local servers or private networks instead of relying on cloud-based systems. This keeps sensitive data secure, reduces reliance on third-party providers and ensures AI tools work even without an internet connection. While it requires more setup and maintenance, it gives businesses full control over their AI processes and data privacy.

Terence has kindly pulled together a list of pros and cons of moving offline:

Pros:

- **Increased privacy.** Queries and files sent to the AI remain in the machine. This includes all custom training.
- **Intellectual property.** Information and data sent to the AI tool can't be misused to train the provider's AI model without your permission.
- **Improved security.** By running AI on a separate, segregated computer, you can cut off internet access to the "AI computer" to ensure nothing external can access the device.

Cons:

- **Requires a powerful computer.** For acceptable performance, you need high-functioning processors, graphics processing units (GPUs) and memory, which mightn't be available on your existing computer. A budget IT setup won't work.

- **Needs a fast internet connection.** Even though it will be offline, you initially need a decent connection to download the AI model, which requires a sufficient amount of storage and internet data download limits.
- **Hard to set up.** Some offline systems can be tricky for the average non-techy computer user to configure. For example, users may struggle with knowing which commands to enter to install, initialise and run the software.
- **Potentially hidden malware.** AI models of the most popular formats can contain executable code, which can put you at risk. Like downloading any software, ensure you're exercising due diligence when downloading AI models.

How do we know AI tools are safe to use?

Personally, I don't push specific tools because it is often difficult to find their origins and level of security. I asked Nakshathra for red flags to look out for to ensure protection:

- **Do they have a good reputation?** Always do your research. Head to Google and search for "[AI Tool] statistics" or "[AI Tool] recent statistics" to uncover recent updates, user demographics and media reports. These sources also highlight lawsuits, ethical concerns and how a platform is trending.
- **What's the defined category?** Online sources often categorise AI usage under different segments, such as work, leisure, art and connectivity. If a tool is also used for adult content, fraud or scams, that's a major concern.
- **Any issues with the terms and conditions?** Many AI startups in Australia lack clear policies, making it difficult for users to understand what data they're giving away. Some startup founders Nakshathra has spoken to aren't even aware of voluntary AI standards.

- **Will it provide misleading information?** Most AI tools claim accuracy, but you need to be aware of hallucinations, aka AI-generated misinformation. A simple way to test an AI tool is to ask it a question within your area of expertise, then demand sources. If it provides misleading references, that's a major issue. Always fact-check AI-generated outputs before trusting them.

That last point is a big one to remember. DeepSeek, a Chinese AI chatbot that's basically China's answer to ChatGPT, has been all the rage since February 2025. But its development and release brought to light massive issues about information control and censorship of "undesirable output". Sensitive topics (well, at least to the Chinese government) like Tiananmen Square and Taiwan prompted responses like, "Sorry, that's beyond my current scope. Let's talk about something else."

It's important to note this isn't hallucination or protected information – it's just straight up censored outputs. Even more importantly, *The Guardian* found it *actually* responded with correct information when asked in a roundabout way (e.g. "Tank Man" instead of dates or places), and discovered if you replace letters with special characters like 3=E, A=4 and S=5 it becomes obvious that DeepSeek has the information, it's just been trained *not* to provide it in plain language in response to specific prompts.

Protecting your data

In March 2024, the European Union (EU) officially approved the *Artificial Intelligence Act (AI Act)* – a legal framework designed to regulate AI systems based on their level of risk. The law sorts AI into four risk categories – unacceptable, high, limited and minimal – with different rules for each. High-risk AI, for example, must pass strict assessments before being used, while certain applications, like biometric mass surveillance, are completely banned. By approving the *AI Act*, the EU has arguably set a global high watermark for AI regulation. While there isn't currently a similar law in Australia, a voluntary set of AI Ethics Principles has existed since 2019.

According to global law firm Dentons, the EU's *AI Act* may act as a de facto standard for the regulation of AI:

> For businesses with a global presence, it may be simpler to adhere to and adopt these more stringent regulations in the EU across all of the regions in which these businesses operate, including in Australia.

In other words, rather than having multiple AI acts across the globe, it would be smoother in most instances for everyone to abide by the same rules.

But whether a local AI act is introduced or not, Terence strongly recommends introducing a hierarchy, similar to the EU's *AI Act*, for your company in the meantime. The hierarchy should clearly define guidelines around mixing company documentation with AI tools. He suggests leaders classify information into levels such as public, restricted and confidential, as follows:

- **Public information** – safe to upload to GenAI tools like ChatGPT.
- **Restricted information** – not confidential but shouldn't be widely shared.
- **Confidential information** – requires secure platforms or internal tools.

These classifications are great for guiding teams on what's safe to share and where, so examples relevant to your company and departments should be outlined in your AI policy (as mentioned in the previous chapter). You need to ensure your team is educated about the risks of AI usage within their role, and compliance around secure practices and sharing particular information is enforced.

To ensure compliance with laws and regulations, Nakshathra highly recommends appointing a Chief AI Officer or dedicated compliance officer to oversee AI-related risks:

You need someone who ensures every single thing the company does with AI is compliant with the laws and regulations. It could be a lawyer, or it could be an independent individual who's able to assess whether something might be an issue in the future. You need to take proactive measures for future-proofing and essentially understanding where a company might be going wrong or might be going right.

Many large companies already have Chief AI Officers, but even small businesses need someone focused on AI compliance and ethics. This role involves monitoring security, assessing privacy risks, evaluating AI tools, and ensuring ethical AI deployment. Without this, companies risk reputational damage and legal repercussions. Investment in compliance software to maintain ethical use is also recommended.

When it comes to protecting the privacy of your employee and client data, you need to obtain ongoing, informed consent explicitly agreeing to how their data will be used. Some GenAI tools allow you to disable training on their data – and we recommend checking that box if possible. With regard to images and photos, Terence says there are some anti-AI tools that are designed to protect against misuse. For example, the Fawkes tool introduces invisible distortions to photos, confusing AI facial recognition systems. It subtly distorts the photo in ways imperceptible to humans. If an AI model trains on those distorted images, it won't correctly recognise the real person later. Artists are using similar tools to protect their work from being scraped and used to train

AI without their permission. With AI evolving, we're likely to see anti-AI solutions for video emerge soon.

Protection against deep fakes, scams and other fraudulent activity

Right now, too many organisations are rushing to implement AI without questioning the potential risks of misuse or whether AI is the right solution. Looking ahead, businesses should prepare for increased cybercrime.

We don't want to freak you out here, but you need to become wary of deepfake scams, which may become commonplace. A deepfake is an AI-generated image, video or audio clip designed to look and sound real – but isn't. Using advanced machine learning, deepfakes can swap faces, mimic voices or create entirely fake scenarios, making it harder to tell what's true online. While they can be fun for entertainment, they also pose serious risks, from misinformation to identity fraud.

According to the Cornell University study *Deepfake detection: Humans vs. machines*, people can accurately identify deepfake facial images only 50% of the time and deepfake faces in videos just 24.5% of the time. And many were just guessing. As the technology evolves, humans will become even easier to deceive. This is not a problem for the future – some deepfake scams are already proving successful. For example, there was a case in Hong Kong in May 2024 where a British multinational design and engineering company was the target of a deepfake scam that led to one of its Hong Kong employees paying out $25 million to fraudsters. According to *CNN Business*, a finance worker was "duped into attending a video call with people he believed were the chief financial officer and other members of staff, but all of whom turned out to be deepfake re-creations".

Terence says that even with AI regulations introduced, stopping deepfakes will be difficult – especially when there are open-source tools that allow anyone to create deepfakes or voice clones. (Such tools allegedly "polluted" the 2024 US presidential election.) Once the knowledge is out there, people can't simply unlearn it.

So, what do we do? The first step is to take a risk-based approach. For low-risk situations, like deciding where to go for lunch, there's no need to worry about deepfakes – the consequences are minimal. But for high-risk situations, like defence or financial transactions, you need stricter measures. In these instances, you may require face-to-face interactions or multi-factor authentication methods, like using passwords agreed upon during in-person meetings to verify someone's identity. (Oh, look at that – traditional communication methods like real-life human interactions could see a major comeback!)

Businesses can also adopt more secure platforms like WhatsApp Business or Apple's iMessage, which use authentication methods that are harder to spoof. While they're not foolproof, they're better than text messaging, which can be easily hacked. But always keep in mind that scammers could very easily register a business name on WhatsApp and impersonate someone you know. While inconvenient, it's essential to double-check phone numbers and verify accounts if you see any unusual messages pop up.

Additional technical solutions are currently being explored. For example, cryptographic signatures are requested to verify that a program hasn't been tampered with. A similar system could be applied to photos or videos, where digital signatures prove their authenticity and trace their origin. However, implementing this on a large scale would require re-engineering cameras, devices and editing software – it will take *a while* to effectively roll this out throughout the world. Regarding emails, there's a new standard called BIMI (Brand Indicators for Message Identification), which allows verified companies to display their logo in your inbox. However, getting certified is an exhaustive process involving identity verification, trademark checks and more.

While it all sounds intense, increased security measures will become essential for building and maintaining trust. Some AI tools have proven useful for detecting abnormalities within large amounts of data that humans would otherwise have great difficulty with. For example, in November 2024 Google successfully pinpointed 26 new vulnerabilities to open-source project maintainers. According to *Forbes*, as far as the researchers could tell, "this vulnerability has likely been present for two decades and wouldn't have been discoverable with existing fuzz targets written by humans". It's great to see a positive use case of AI in action!

Final thoughts...

Rather than sitting there in denial, we all must stay informed and adopt a layered security approach in this new AI-infused world.

Without a doubt, developing clear policies, educating our teams and embracing tools that prioritise privacy and security is absolutely key to ensure our companies remain protected. Above all else, we always need to remain sceptical in the face of possible deepfakes and scams. Healthy scepticism is one of the best defences.

We look forward to watching security and privacy regulations and software improve in the near future.

AI-generated chapter summary *(with human tweaks)*

- AI security risks are growing. GenAI tools can inadvertently expose sensitive data, making privacy and security a top concern for businesses.

- Sensitive data should be handled cautiously. If a piece of information would cause a crisis if leaked, it should not be uploaded to AI tools.

- AI tools hosted under US jurisdiction, such as OpenAI's ChatGPT and Microsoft Copilot, may be subject to the *USA PATRIOT Act*, raising legal and regulatory concerns about data privacy.

- AI tools mix user data and commands, making them susceptible to prompt injection attacks that could lead to leaks or exploitation.

- There is a growing threat of deepfakes and misinformation. AI-generated deepfakes are becoming more sophisticated, with real-world scams already leading to major financial losses.

- Businesses should consider building a secure AI environments, such as private AI platforms, local offline models, and strictly classify data into public, restricted and confidential categories.

- Appointing a Chief AI Officer or compliance officer ensures responsible AI use, risk assessment and adherence to emerging regulations like the *EU AI Act*.

- Proactively implementing security measures such as cryptographic signatures, multi-factor authentication and AI-specific risk policies can help safeguard organisations from emerging cyber threats.

- Education is key. Organisations must prioritise AI literacy, training employees on security best practices and the ethical use of AI tools to mitigate risks effectively.

PART IV

TACTICAL STRATEGY

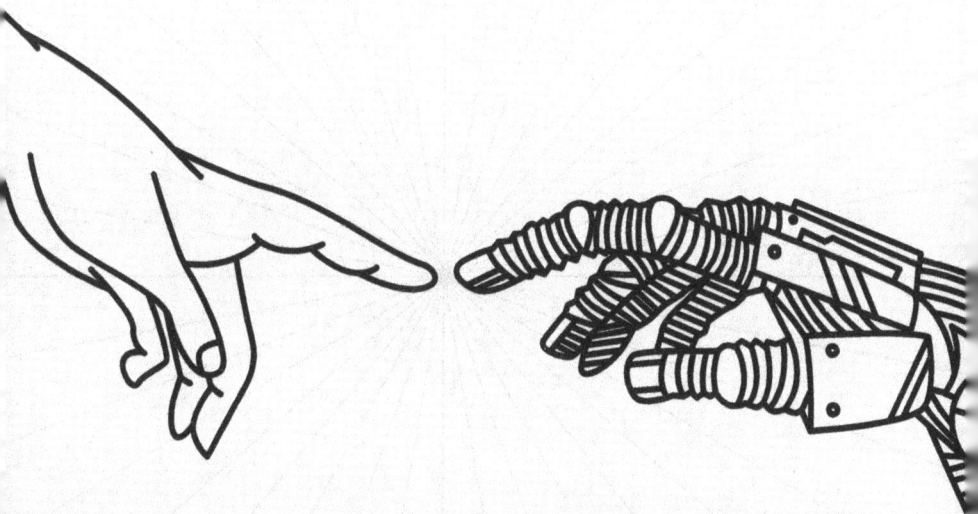

Chapter 14

Building an AI-ready Team Culture

"Leaders today don't just want success –
they want balance, sustainability and fulfilment.
AI can support that if we use it wisely."

Vanessa (Ness) Medling

Recently, I sat down with a small marketing team and asked them about their biggest AI challenges right now. One of the members instantly shared her frustrations about the poorly formed AI-generated briefs her manager was passing around. She said the instructions were too hard to decipher and it always took her ages to fully understand the requirements. In the end, she had to create her own human-generated version of the brief before diving into the project. As you can imagine, this was extremely annoying and time-consuming.

Her experiences reminded me of a time in early 2023 when I was editing monthly articles for a client. ChatGPT had been around for a few months by then, and I'd started to see a shift in style in the content that landed in my inbox for review. Yep, you guessed it – my client had started handing over the writing process to AI.

Feeling conflicted between only being paid to edit versus wanting to pass back high-quality articles for publication, I usually rewrote whole sections to add more depth to the surface-level content. It wasn't fantastic, but I had to value my time. I admit to never building up the guts to address the issue with my client, though.

Both scenarios are classic examples of leaders handing over tasks to the bots without fully comprehending the repercussions. I don't blame them though, because they were obviously looking for ways to be more productive with their time and AI was *right there* for the taking. As mentioned throughout the book, this is a trap you need to avoid. Because while using GenAI might save you time up front, it has the potential to create lengthy tasks that take your team longer than necessary to complete on the other side. In other words, *you* might be more productive, but you're actually *adding* to your team's workload.

In this chapter, I address ways you can positively lead your team to effective AI implementation. It involves putting them into the right headspace, offering continual support and asking for continual feedback. As a leader, this is your responsibility. It's up to you to think about, act and lead rationally with regard to AI's place within your team to ensure a positive, human-first work culture. To support me with the following pages, I approached leadership coaches and co-authors of *Healthy Hustle: The New Blueprint to Thrive in Business and Life* Nicky Miklos-Woodley and Ness Medling. They had so many insights to share about this subject, which helped form the basis of the chapter. Thanks so much for your help, ladies!

Embracing AI effectively as a leader

With this book under your belt, you should be way past the AI avoidance phase. You're feeling more confident about smoothly integrating AI into your business's day-to-day tasks with the human touch, while also being wary about the ethical, legal, security and privacy aspects. Now it's time to bring your team along for the ride.

Apart from buying them all a copy of *AI-Human Fusion* (which, of course, I highly recommend!), you need to lead by example. This involves setting up the best practices and processes to provide a holistic understanding of AI, as well as a sense of job security given the somewhat unknown future of this fast-moving world.

As wonderfully summed up by Nicky, there are two spectrums of leadership when it comes to AI: "Some over-rely on it and lose the human element. Others are so busy they don't even think about using it meaningfully." The key here is to pause for a moment and consider the following questions:

- How can we use AI to build a thriving culture?
- How can we integrate it to create amazing operating rhythms?
- Are we using it to build foundational structures like position descriptions and job scopes without relying on it too much?
- How can we use it to upskill our people?

Since GenAI exploded onto the scene, I've seen and heard about too many knee-jerk reactions. Jumping onto AI for the sake of "keeping ahead of the curve". Throwing money at tools with technical maturity equivalent to disobedient, tantruming toddlers. And sending out the firing squad before giving teams the chance to upskill or transition internally. In reality, we need to empower our human team members and work through this transition slowly, rather than simply dumping new technology on them or eradicating them completely.

Avoiding AI over-reliance

Even though I'm writing a book about AI, I've been extremely conscious about not allowing myself to over-rely on the technology at any point. With the knowledge that ChatGPT can now capture my personal brand voice extremely well, it would've been so easy to just ask the bot to draft full chapters for me. But I didn't want to go down the path of over-reliance. I wanted to proudly send *AI-Human Fusion* into the world knowing that it was at least 90% written by me. Otherwise, I'd wind up feeling like a fraud.

Have you found yourself turning to AI a little too frequently for your liking? I totally get it. But, somehow, you need to dig deep and ensure a healthy human brain versus AI ratio. While the technology is still evolving, this ratio might be 90:10, or possibly 80:20. As mentioned in earlier chapters, if we want humanity to thrive in an AI world, we can't afford to become lazy and let those left numbers drop too low. I know I might sound like a broken record here, but the bots can never fully replace your unique thinking. AI can't match your experience, gut instincts or creativity. This is why, as a leader, you must constantly review AI output and encourage your team to do the same.

If you or anyone in your team is feeling time-poor, burnt out or struggling with self-doubt, they're likely to skip this step – and that's when the AI output and outcomes go off track. Unfortunately, over-reliance on AI typically happens when in this headspace. If this is already occurring or occurs in the future within your team, it might be a clue that it's time for everyone to pause and reflect – and potentially seek mental health support if it's an ongoing area of concern.

Ness advises that it's all about using AI with intention: "If we just use AI to speed up our to-do list, we're missing the point. The real question is, 'How do we use AI to create more time for what truly matters?" In their book, Nicky and Ness talk about a concept called "busy versus living". Being busy is chaotic – that "go, go, go" mindset – while living means being present in the moment and creating space. They advise that AI can actually be useful for moving us from "busy" to "living".

For example, you can use AI to:

- spark creativity when you're feeling blocked
- help brainstorm new ideas for workshops, games or team engagement
- handle basic administration tasks that drain your energy but still need to be done.

AI can be a great virtual assistant, giving you back time for the things that truly matter, like focusing on your leadership, creativity and wellbeing. But is that what you're doing? If AI assistance gave you a few extra hours in your day, would you use that "free" time to build stronger relationships with colleagues and clients, brainstorm new strategies and incentives to enhance team results, or go home on time for once? Or, would you use that "free" time to cram in more unnecessary meetings or emails, scroll on social media or experiment with the latest shiny AI tool? Ness wisely says, "If you don't replace time with something meaningful, you'll unconsciously fill it with more work".

To avoid over-reliance, remember this little line:

*While AI can create positive space, humans will always have a place.**

And if you ever find yourself fighting with your GenAI tool because it doesn't produce the outcome you want, maybe it's time to step away with a notepad and do some good old-fashioned human critical thinking.

---

* My human brain literally just came up with that gold nugget. Maybe I should turn it into the office equivalent of bumper stickers...

Hear from the humans
Jasmin Hyde, Founding Director at Hyde & Seek Communications

The over-reliance on AI is an important conversation, especially as tools become more ingrained in daily workflows. While AI can obviously enhance efficiency, creativity and problem-solving when used well, we must remember that it's still a tool (albeit a powerful one). It will never be a be-all replacement for human intuition, judgement and critical thinking.

Creating intentional space for independent thinking and problem-solving may seem obvious, but it's an increasingly vital practice to avoid over-reliance on AI and stay sharp. Some strategies include the following:

- **Cut down usage.** Dedicate one day a week (or even a few hours each day) to work without AI tools. This can help refresh your cognitive abilities, encourage innovative thinking and re-engage the mind, making you more creative and agile.

- **Use AI as an enhancer, not a crutch.** Support and refine core skills by working with the tool as a sounding board for ideas or finalising your content.

- **Strengthen skills that technology can't replace.** Reading books, engaging in face-to-face communication and taking part in hands-on activities are all "offline" practices that improve problem-solving and encourage deeper thinking.

- **Prioritise critical and strategic decision-making by humans.** Using AI for repetitive, time-consuming tasks is fine, but AI doesn't have the human capacity for empathy, ethical judgement or nuanced understanding.

- **Regularly assess how AI tools are being used.** Are they improving efficiency without undermining personal development or creativity? Reflecting on your AI habits can help you strike a healthier balance.

By establishing a mindful relationship with AI and prioritising regular breaks from it, we can maintain our cognitive resilience and creative edge while still benefiting from the efficiency AI brings.

Ensuring a human-first culture

I'm hearing many stories from employed friends and family members about being asked to return to the office more often rather than working from home, now that the pandemic is a distant memory. And how annoying it is. And unproductive. But just like in the AI world, we shouldn't be prioritising productivity over real-life human interactions. Going into the office to be present with your team *shouldn't* be a burden. Yes, there will be times when you just need to get sh*t done, and it's better to do it from your tranquil home office or kitchen bench. But it's not healthy to do it all the time.

I recently saw a LinkedIn post from my friend David Jeffery, Director of Technology at the recruitment company Reo Group, that grabbed my attention. He shared an inspiring experience from a particular day in the office as a reminder of what being in the office alongside your peers can do for you:

Amid the usual buzz and activity, one conversation stood out. For 15 minutes, I had the privilege of hearing one of our consultants turn a NO into a YES through a combination of facts, evidence, business acumen, and industry insights, all while keeping the client's best interests at heart. It was a true display of professionalism that captured my full attention. Had I been sitting at home I would have missed the experience entirely and learned nothing.

Moral of the story: as much as I know you love working from home, NOTHING can compete with the osmosis of being in the office. Even after 20 years in this industry, moments like these remind me that learning never stops and the value of observing excellence firsthand is something no training can replicate.

David's encounter doesn't just show the power of being physically in the office; it also highlights the beauty of human connection via the formation of a mutually respectful client relationship. From my perspective, as an entrepreneur who's hustled from home for years, there's a reason I've invested in an office at a local co-working space: I enjoy bumping into and bonding with humans every now and again. It reminds me there's a whole world out there...

Hear from the humans
Vanessa 'Ness' Medling, Leadership Coach at Business Together

Generally speaking, we're human beings interacting with other human beings. Leaders are there to create an environment and a culture for the team to thrive in. If we have a bunch of human beings at work, then we need to have that human-first component, because people need connection. They need a sense of belonging, a sense of purpose.

During the whole COVID situation with people working remotely, leaders had to find ways to manage their teams remotely. What many of their teams were missing was that human interaction. For those who were introverted and like being in their own space, they thrived. But leaders found it really difficult to lead their teams, because they had to be creative in how they connected with and created that sense of team cohesion and belonging.

In my view, it's no different to AI, because we need to bring people together for a common purpose, a common vision. People need to understand what their role is in achieving that vision. They need to pour their heart and soul into something to be able to go and deliver above and beyond. So I just think it's really dangerous to go down the track of wanting an AI-first business. It will create a repeat of the challenges that leaders had in COVID. You can't just go, "Don't worry about the people. We've got the AI and we're good to go".

If we did, then who's out there checking for mistakes?

Slow and steady team implementation

Okay, Leanne. We're keen to enhance our team's productivity with AI. So, how do we do that effectively without becoming lazy and still keep it human?

Oh, I'm so glad you asked! From my experience, teams usually feature a mix of excitement, confusion and a little fear when it comes to AI, falling into one of the following categories:

- The **innovators** who play with all the AI tools but potentially misuse them or spend too much time on them.
- The **dabblers** who log into GenAI now and then but are unsure what they're doing.
- The **worriers** who completely freak out and still haven't set up any AI accounts.

As long as you've got people wildly using AI with no direction, and others completely avoiding it, it's almost impossible to find a way for AI to serve your team properly. The first thing you need to do is work out a middle ground to get them on the same page.

Establishing a clear AI policy (as mentioned in Chapter 12: Protect Your Business, Protect Your IP) is a great start – but you can't just dump a copy on every desk or flick out an email advising employees a soft copy is available on the server for them to read and start implementing at their earliest convenience. You need to actively lead everyone by organising programs and processes if you truly want to enhance everyone's creativity, deepen relationships and drive sustainable growth.

Supportive AI team discussions

If you haven't already, I suggest bringing your team together for monthly open discussions about AI. Encourage everyone to share their thoughts, fears and concerns. This is an opportunity to dispel any misconceptions about AI being too complex or threatening job security.

I recommend facilitating transparent conversations about how AI can align with your team's goals. Discuss the ways it can make daily tasks easier, free up time for more creative work and even enhance personal job satisfaction. By involving everyone, you establish a collaborative approach where the team feels ownership over AI adoption, rather than seeing it as an external force imposed upon them. You also need everyone to be crystal clear on why AI is being used and what the expected outcome is.

Promote the idea that AI isn't here to replace their roles. Remind them it's here to help make them more efficient and impactful. Setting the right tone in these meetings can create a supportive environment for experimentation.

Nicky and Ness suggest having one team member champion AI each month, meaning they're responsible for researching what's new in the AI world and sharing insights. It makes AI adaptation more engaging and stops people from falling behind. This works better than expecting everyone to figure it out on their own or always having the same AI enthusiast put their hand up for the task rather than focusing on more meaningful work. In addition, it feeds into other developmental opportunities. For example, when someone presents their findings to the team, it enables them to improve their presentation skills.

During these meetings, it's ideal to set and review measurable AI goals. This allows you to track the effectiveness of AI to understand its impact on your team and company. Define clear, measurable goals such as the amount of time saved or increases in engagement rates due to AI-driven initiatives. For example, you might measure how long a task took before and after implementing AI, or track improvements in campaign performance. This data-driven approach allows you to tweak AI usage and demonstrate its benefits to the team, reinforcing that AI is enhancing productivity, not replacing human creativity.

Tailored training plans

After getting a good grasp of your team's AI needs, I recommend developing an ongoing tailored training plan that builds their understanding and skills progressively. As Nicky highlights, "AI changes so rapidly, you can't just do one session and assume people are set for life. You need a long-term strategy". She says a plan should include:

- structured training on how to use AI effectively
- regular coaching to ensure the tool is being used the right way
- clear expectations so AI isn't just thrown in for the sake of it.

While your team doesn't need to dive into complex algorithms or coding, knowing the essentials will help everyone feel more in control. It's a bit like learning to drive: you don't need to know how the engine works, but you do need to understand how to use the steering wheel, pedals and indicators to feel confident and remain safe on the road.

Your tailored training plan might include organising in-house AI interactive workshops, programs or keynotes, or investing in tickets to upcoming AI conferences and summits in your area. You could also seek online programs or books (hint, hint) that team members can chip away at over a few weeks. If you have budget constraints, you can even start smaller than that – like sourcing YouTube tutorials, podcasts or TikToks.

My only advice is to do your due diligence and have a few people look into the viability and quality of the content. I've witnessed firsthand some dodgy, AI-generated videos and books, and I've heard about bot-produced online courses released by prestigious educational institutions. Like in life, there's nothing better than human referrals and recommendations.

Throughout the training process, there need to be regular check-ins to see how everyone is tracking and refine the training plans accordingly. This is how you can ensure AI integration becomes a natural part of your culture.

Experimentation with low-risk tasks

I see too many organisations throwing themselves into big projects too soon and overinvesting in AI tools that are only in their infancy. Rather than rushing into using AI for high-stakes campaigns or tackling that massive project that's been on the to-do list for years, start by experimenting with simple, low-risk tasks – ideally, tasks that are already implemented on a regular basis, like using GenAI to brainstorm ideas for your next project or draft an email to a disgruntled customer that you've been putting off.

By starting with simple, everyday tasks, your team will get a sense of how AI works without feeling like they're diving into the deep end. Each small win builds confidence and opens the door to bigger possibilities. Just continually remind them to review absolutely everything AI produces. *(Yes, Leanne. I know, I know...)* Once they've gained hands-on experience with effective prompt engineering and seen the results, they'll feel more comfortable expanding its usage.

The tool debate

Wherever I go, I'm asked about the best AI tools to use for various purposes. However, I'm always wary about making recommendations when all tools are in their infancy right now, with many posing potential security threats. I'm also wary about collating a pile of shiny objects to play with when the majority of leaders and teams are experiencing general overwhelm and already have a scrambled collection of to-do items scribbled on post-it notes across their desk.

Here's the hard-hitting reality: if your team isn't currently being productive *without* AI, it's key to assess and address the situation before introducing new shiny tools. Because you'll need to source, experiment with and implement these tools. And that all takes time – possibly unnecessary time. Before bringing in AI tools, it's essential to first stop and agree upon the problems you're trying to solve and what you actually need AI to do. As Ness advises, you "otherwise end up with 'cool tool of the week' syndrome – where people get excited about random AI gimmicks that aren't actually useful".

The irony is that AI is often seen as the solution to enhanced productivity, but it can also be productivity's enemy.

Establishment of a buddy system

I believe it's important to pull members together to explore AI as a team. A buddy system reduces the intimidation factor for existing non-AI-action-takers by matching them up with more tech-comfy colleagues to share their experiences, troubleshoot issues and brainstorm ways to make the most of the technology.

This system also creates a beautiful learning culture within your team. People are more likely to try new things when they have a partner by their side to share insights. As AI can often feel like unfamiliar territory, learning in pairs is a great way to promote support and creative problem-solving.

You might even like to take it a step further by setting up cross-department buddy systems. Even though the day-to-day tasks might be different, successful prompt strategies for one human might lead to lightbulb moments for another. There's so much potential here to enhance critical and creative thinking with AI as the subject matter.

Hackathons

Here's a fun idea for you to introduce: hackathons. They can be a game-changer for getting teams hands-on with AI in a way that's fun, practical and actually drives results. Instead of passively learning about AI, participants jump straight into real-world projects, with mentoring and live demos to guide them. The best ones have a mix of structured learning, team challenges, and a final showcase where ideas are pitched to leadership – proving AI's value in action. By making AI feel tangible (and a little competitive), hackathons can upskill teams while also creating a ripple effect of innovation across the business.

Hear from the humans
Nicole Hilgenkamp, AI Consultant at Alboration LLC

My best hack for ensuring a human-in-the-loop approach is to empower people with AI skills. Knowledgeable workers are best positioned to use AI to streamline their work, and by doing so, they free up capacity for further upskilling in AI-driven processes.

I reinforce this by leveraging "hackathons" as a scalable enablement tool – equipping large groups with AI skills while also inspiring them to actively engage in further AI advancement as they gain expertise.

Why do hackathons? Well, businesses and organisations see an increased employee engagement with understanding emerging technologies, like AI, through hands-on initiatives. A hackathon helps leaders encourage early adoption of technology (i.e. AI tools) by providing baseline knowledge and training in a controlled environment. This includes training of policies and procedures, AI applications of choice for AI, the risk, and company expectations using the AI in their company or business.

This works for business as well. It gives them a reason for hands-on experiences to help achieve a return on investment in the technology, allowing workplace problems or redundancies to be solved through AI use cases. This includes potential scaling opportunities.

Final thoughts...

Implementing an effective team protocol for AI use is the biggest step to making AI work in your business. After all, you can't just rely on the tools themselves to have an impact. It all comes down to how AI is overseen and managed by the actual experts in your business.

The problem-solving and creative skills of free-thinking, responsive humans can't successfully complement the power of AI without systems and processes in place. Like everything in the working world, success comes from adapting to change and minimising the risks and fail points. AI is no different.

AI-generated chapter summary *(with human tweaks)*

- AI should enhance, not complicate. Leaders must be intentional, ensuring AI supports workflows rather than adding frustration or inefficiencies.

- Balance is key. Over-reliance on AI can weaken human creativity and critical thinking. The right mix of AI and human input keeps work meaningful and effective.

- AI should create space, not just speed. The goal isn't just to do more but to free up time for creativity, collaboration and high-value work.

- Clear expectations, ongoing training and open discussions help teams integrate AI confidently rather than feeling overwhelmed.

- Track AI success through efficiency gains, cost savings and improved workflows to prove its value and refine adoption strategies.

- Hackathons drive real AI adoption. Hands-on events allow teams to experiment, build AI skills and develop real-world use cases, creating lasting momentum.

Chapter 15

Future-proofing with AI literacy

"I believe AI is here to stay and this is
only the beginning of its journey!"

Beckie Lee

As I write this, it's 5.30 am and I'm sitting on my couch, in my pyjamas, on manuscript deadline day. As teachers say to school kids, let's give ourselves a big pat on the back! Right now, you and I are in a similar mindset as *AI-Human Fusion* draws to a close – the only difference is that you're reading these pages while I'm writing them. However, despite this being the last official chapter of this book, your AI education does not and should not stop here.

We're only at the 10% mark of AI's future potential. I don't say this to scare you, but more to prepare you. The technology is only going to continue to evolve and improve. It's going to mature from the toddler stage to the kindergartener stage to the teenage stage… until it becomes the equivalent of a fully-fledged adult. It's going to keep making mistakes, but it will also keep learning from the human brains around it. At some point, AI will be completely integrated within our lives – in the same way no one blinks an eyelid when someone says "internet" or "electricity" these days. It will just be something that naturally co-exists with us. I particularly look forward to the day when I have my very own housekeeper, like Rosey the Robot from *The Jetsons*, meaning my home will finally have some sort of order. (Unfortunately, I'm just as bad as the kids…)

Whatever the future looks like, it's up to you, as a busy human leader, to stay in control. Understand what you're working with and dealing with. Develop positive habits to ensure your brain continues to buzz with activity rather than lounge around like a couch potato. Whether this book kickstarted your AI literacy or continued it, I urge you to consider your next steps for you and your team. Based on everything you've read throughout these pages, some of my suggested next steps include:

- buying everyone a copy of this book (and keeping them accountable to read it)
- establishing an AI policy
- looking into security and privacy measures
- setting up monthly AI discussion meetings
- establishing tailored training plans

And, most of all:

- **ensuring your humans are still running the show.**

If you take away *anything* from this book, please make it that last step.

Why is AI literacy so vital?

Going forward, companies won't be hiring based on how many hours people have spent tinkering with AI tools. They'll be looking for people who can think critically about AI, use it strategically and push it to deliver improved results.

On a few occasions, I've heard people mention that school leavers are better off studying degrees in art or philosophy – subjects that make them think – rather than those based on memorising facts, like medicine and law. Because at some point, AI will hallucinate less frequently and become more reliable for factual information, and it will then come down to humans to use our own critical thinking, emotional intelligence, experiences and gut instincts to work with the AI output to come up with quality, trustworthy solutions. Remember, AI is just a tool to enhance our experience and expertise.

The secret to AI literacy isn't chasing every update or jumping onto every new tool. It's:

- understanding AI's strengths and limitations so you can use it with intention
- developing the skills to guide AI rather than letting it guide you
- becoming adaptable, so no matter how AI evolves, you maintain mental clarity, remain confident in your ability to work with it and stay in control.

The strongest professionals will be those who can direct AI with purpose, question its outputs and blend their own expertise with machine-generated insights. By sharpening your critical thinking and strategic approach, you can be among those leading the way in AI's evolution.

Jumping onboard the training train

I've come a long way since that first webinar on "How to use ChatGPT and still sound human". As mentioned, it quickly led to me speaking at numerous conferences, summits and networking events. It was initially all extremely reactive – almost like someone had flung a lasso around my neck, pulling me this way and that.

Hey, don't get me wrong, I absolutely loved the experience, but I knew I had to start being more proactive.

For a few months, I co-hosted a podcast, *The AI Train*, with fellow copywriter and AI enthusiast Tim King, which really helped build my confidence around talking about AI off the cuff. Then, in March 2024, I launched The AI DIY Club – a low-cost online membership model for microbusiness-owners, offering weekly DIY training sessions and Q&As. But after seven months, I closed it up. While I had a handful of keen club VIPs showing up each week, I felt I needed to go bigger and make a greater impact. I had pulled together all this awesome content for literally three people every time.

I knew I had to stop playing small and move into the corporate space. I started working with Mehri Doyle as my Learning and Development Mentor and developed a few strategies and materials. I also joined Janine Garner's Elevate mastermind and moved out of my home office, which helped me "level-up" my mindset. Not long after that, I received the exciting news that Major Street Publishing was interested in the concept of *AI-Human Fusion*. And here it is in your hands.

While working on my personal and business development behind the scenes, I've helped many entrepreneurs and teams with their AI understanding. These days, my core focuses are delivering keynotes, and half- and full-day one-on-one and team workshops. Nothing lights me up more than witnessing the a-ha moments and game-changing learnings of the participants. I truly feel I've found my place in this world.

Do I recommend AI training for you and your team? Well, of course I do! To put it simply, the AI space has massive potential, and most people are struggling to stumble their way through it. However, it seems many companies are putting training "on hold for now", and this concerns me. Now is actually the perfect time to jump on board. Wouldn't it be easier to get your head around it when it's still in its infancy and grow alongside it? If you were to learn a new language, wouldn't you feel more comfortable hanging out with a toddler, who's still developing their vocabulary themselves, versus feeling completely lost in conversation with a university professor?

According to a 2024 survey by HR consultancy Randstad, even though 75% of companies have adopted AI technology, only 35% of employees received AI training in the last year. Interestingly, just 22% of Baby Boomers and 28% of Gen X were offered AI skilling opportunities, compared to 45% of Gen Z and 43% of Millennials. I know older individuals are closer to retirement age, but I don't think that matters at all – everyone needs to be learning about AI, regardless of age. It's critical for people of all ages and walks of life to embrace it, understand it and discuss it. Call me an AI nerd, but I believe the varying perspectives lead to super insightful conversations.

Randstad CEO, Sander van 't Noordende, was quoted as saying, "Talent scarcity is a significant global challenge, and so equitable access to skilling, resources and opportunities needs to be a fundamental part of addressing this. However, when it comes to AI, demand continues to grow at an unprecedented rate, and so does the AI equity gap it is creating."

He continues to say that unless we recognise this issue and take active steps to address it, the pool of workers prepared for the future of working within the AI world will be too small – creating even more job shortages across industries in the long run.

And I agree. I also agree with Randstad's key recommendations for organisations to promote equitable AI adoption. These include the following:

- **Improving skills.** Organisations must adopt faster, more inclusive skilling approaches. This will help ensure all demographics are able to keep up with the rapidly evolving AI technologies.

- **Exploring possibilities and limitations.** Companies must critically assess both the potential and limitations of AI, including the review of potential biases and ensuring staff are well prepared to use AI effectively.

- **Taking a personalised approach.** Employers should be across the unique barriers different groups face in AI adoption and be open to developing opportunities and programs to meet these diverse needs.

- **Encouraging collaboration.** Partnerships between businesses, educational institutions and local organisations are essential to help bridge AI skills gaps and ensure long-term equity across all demographics.

Your team probably knows they should be using AI to simplify processes and elevate content, but without proper guidance, it's easy to get stuck in a cycle of trial and error. The whole concept of AI then becomes stressful and inefficient, and leads to missed opportunities. Training flips the script. It ensures your team isn't just testing random prompts and hoping for the best but actually crafting outputs that are on brand, high quality and efficient. It also brings everyone onto the same page, removing the guesswork and building a collective confidence that AI is working for you, not creating more work.

What quality training looks like

The best type of AI training should offer practical, human-centric learning that provides real-world skills you and your team can put to work immediately. This is my core focus at HumanEdge AI Training.

Whether you choose to work with me or go elsewhere, you want to look out for training that:

- **Isn't heavily tool-focused.** I know it's tempting to sign up for training that promises to cover the "latest and greatest" AI tools out there. But while there are some very cool options in the library of 18,000 AI tools, there are no guarantees any particular tool will be around in six months' time (or less!). The last thing you want to do is invest in training that covers a series of tools that will potentially be obsolete in the near future. Having said that, training on the big players like ChatGPT, Copilot and Gemini is a somewhat safer option as they're unlikely to be going anywhere anytime soon. I recommend prioritising a provider who teaches core skills like prompt engineering, critical thinking and practical strategies over flashy demonstrations.

- **Encourages practical application.** No one learns by sitting through endless slides of technical jargon. You want to look for training that skips the abstract theory and creates opportunities to be hands-on. I believe it's the only way to truly understand AI's opportunities and limitations. You and your team should leave the session with skills that can be applied to real-world scenarios straight away, like interactive exercises, live demonstrations and practice projects.

- **Justifies the investment.** Sure, everyone loves a bargain. But when it comes to AI training, the cheapest option often cuts corners. While low-cost online programs are okay, they usually include pre-recorded or generic sessions, with limited or no opportunities to work with the trainer for customised solutions. You want to focus on value, including effectiveness and efficiency. Ask yourself if the investment will leave your team feeling swiftly confident and capable, or if it will result in more confusion.

- **Provides ongoing support.** Training shouldn't end when the session does – especially in this constantly evolving AI space. The right provider will ensure you and your team don't just walk away with knowledge; you'll also have the resources to apply it effectively over time. Look for a provider who offers follow-up resources, Q&A opportunities or additional support sessions to show they're invested in your long-term success. Bonus points if they include an evaluation at the end of the formal training to assess your team's progress, identify remaining gaps and recommend tailored next steps. A strong wrap-up ensures the training sticks and delivers real results.

Choosing the right AI training provider shouldn't feel like rocket science (or AI science, for that matter). The right AI training should leave you all feeling fired up and ready to put AI to work – not scratching your heads wondering what to do next. It should give you the clarity to cut through the noise, the confidence to experiment and the know-how to turn AI into a powerful asset for your team.

What some of my students are saying

Yep, I'm going to take a self-indulgent moment right here and share some of the raving reviews from my past students. After all, it's always better to hear it directly from the source...

We had an incredible experience with HumanEdge AI Training! Our custom-designed course was well-structured, engaging, and packed with practical insights that make AI feel accessible and actionable. Leanne is extremely knowledgeable and truly invested in helping participants apply AI in real-world scenarios. The team walked away with a deeper understanding of AI tools and strategies that they could immediately implement in their work. Highly recommended for anyone looking to upskill in AI and stay ahead in the rapidly evolving digital landscape.

Rhys Lawson, Rethink Investing (two-month AI program)

I had the absolute pleasure of working with Leanne as my AI trainer, and the experience was nothing short of transformative. Her depth of knowledge in AI is impressive, but what truly sets her apart is her ability to break down complex concepts into understandable, actionable insights.

Leanne tailored each session to my specific needs and learning pace, ensuring I always felt supported and confident in applying what I learned. Her passion for AI is infectious, and I left every session inspired. If you're looking to truly understand AI and unlock its potential, I can't recommend Leanne enough!

Thank you, Leanne, for being an incredible guide on this journey and adding a new skill to my toolbox!

Margaret King (The AI DIY Club)

I had an excellent experience with Leanne at HumanEdge AI Training. She provided me with valuable insights on how to maximise the use of ChatGPT for my business. Leanne is not only incredibly knowledgeable but also patient, approachable and a natural at teaching. Her personalised tips were easy to follow and immediately useful. I highly recommend her to anyone looking to understand AI better and achieve effective results. Thank you, Leanne!

Julie O'Donovan, Wonsie (one-on-one training)

Leanne presented a session to my group of interior designers about how to use ChatGPT in a clever yet authentic way. Minds were BLOWN! Even if you think you know how to use it, Leanne really digs deeper, and her presentation was excellent.

Lauren Li, Sisalla Interior Design (networking webinar)

Final thoughts...

Now you've pushed past the AI overwhelm, it's time to also say goodbye to those past feelings of being unprepared, unclear and unskilled. With this book and the accompanying online resources (see the QR code or link provided on page vi), you should be feeling much more prepared, purposeful and progressive. *This* is the best positive headspace to be in to effectively and efficiently tap into the productivity opportunities at play – while still ensuring a human-first approach.

As a leader, people are looking to you for direction. Now you have more clarity around AI and the AI-Fusion HABITS framework, you're in a great position to guide them *properly*. Not just throw Microsoft Copilot at them and tell them to "just use it to do stuff quicker". If you and your staff need any further support, remember my team at HumanEdge AI Training and I are here for you. Because you don't have to be the expert yourself. You just have to be the one brave enough to explore.

AI-generated chapter summary *(with human tweaks)*

- AI is here to stay. It's still in its early stages, but like the internet, it will soon be fully integrated into daily life.
- Businesses need AI-literate teams. Companies won't just hire AI users – they'll seek professionals who think critically, apply AI strategically and enhance its outputs.
- AI won't replace human expertise. Judgement, emotional intelligence and real-world experience will remain essential in making AI-generated insights valuable and trustworthy.
- Training should prioritise skills, not tools. AI tools change, but skills like prompt engineering and strategic thinking last.

- Without training, AI creates more confusion than clarity. A lack of guidance leads to inefficiency, wasted time and inconsistent results.
- Investing in training builds confidence and capability. The right training ensures AI works for you, not the other way around.
- Future-proof your team. Those who embrace AI literacy now will lead the way as AI continues to evolve.

Epilogue

The Human Behind the Book

"AI should enhance us, not replace us."

Leanne Shelton

I always knew I wanted to write a book one day. I just didn't know what it would be about. While I enjoyed writing short stories throughout primary school, in later years I realised I'd never have the patience to map out the structure and flesh out the details required for a decent fiction book. Sure, I had a few non-fiction ideas percolating, but up until 12 months ago I'd never predicted that I'd produce an educational resource about one of the biggest technological transitions of our generation. But here it is. All my learnings, musings and rants have manifested into the realisation of a lifelong dream. You're holding that dream in your hands. It has my name on it. I'm now officially an author.

Now, before you ask the question, I'll give you the answer: I wrote this book myself, with my own human brain. I also personally interviewed and extracted information from human experts across various industries around the globe. For anyone supplying written responses, I specifically requested they come from the heart, not the bots. I'm truly grateful for the incredible input received from these experts, as well as other human leaders who were keen to contribute to the conversation. While not everyone I spoke to ended up in the final version, they all contributed in meaningful and lasting ways. I've learnt a lot from them, and I hope you've learnt from those within these pages as well.

The transparent curtain

Although I avoided it as much as possible, I admit to turning to my ChatGPT at times. Most of the time it was because I was completely stuck on how to start a section. Other times, I was curious to see what playful chapter headings it could come up with. Whatever the case, for full transparency I captured almost every single prompt used throughout authoring this book and made them easily accessible via the *AI-Human Fusion* online resources: see the QR code or link provided on page vi. There you can find all my brainstorming, editing, transcript tidying, quote extracting, research assessment, chapter summaries, arguments with the bot to do better... every single bit of it. Throughout it all, I treated my ChatGPT with respect and kindness as my handy virtual assistant. The bot didn't always get things right, but it always provided a useful nudge in the right direction. And it was never my intention to make the bot the writer – because that's my job here, as well as my passion and professional qualification!

Since the start of 2025, I've had a real-life in-house assistant in addition to my virtual one. When it came down to the final compilation of this manuscript and moments of exasperation, he provided human support unmatched by any accessible technological tool. It's a perfect reminder that humans can never truly be replaced.

The human brain is quirky and beautiful

Over the past few years, there has been a shift in thinking around neurodiversity. We've seen the positive emergence of words like "neurospicy" and "superpowers", which are terms I both appreciate and relate to. But above all else, I love the push for empowerment among the neurodiverse community – especially how it celebrates the uniqueness of humans.

Diagnosed with ADHD only 18 months ago (yes, right in the middle of my AI journey), I'm still finding ways to properly understand and accept the ways of my neurospicy brain. While I know neurodiversity can be seen as a magical blessing for some and a curse for others, I'm lucky to say it's been mostly a good thing for me. For starters, I highly doubt I would have thrown myself into a major business pivot like this if it weren't for the excitable sparks shooting off ideas and possibilities left, right and centre within my mind.

But my curious and somewhat wacky brain makes me different from a computer. I mightn't be as fast (although I'm faster than some), accurate (don't ask me for directions) or knowledgeable (but I do my best), but my human brain is what makes me, me. While AI can do amazing things, if it wrote this whole book for me, I would have deprived myself of the tingly sense of achievement that I'm feeling right now. And it's this, the feeling of being a human as I finalise my manuscript, that truly matters in life. Sure, I've had AI assistance, but I'm the one standing on top. *That* is the ideal AI-human fusion.

Final thoughts...

Just before I started writing this book, I removed all social media except LinkedIn (for professional reasons) from my phone. Before long, the constant ego-driven need to check my feed for reactions or comments and the bored, mindless social scrolling was gone. The result? Clarity. Feeling more present, I was able to see human habits more objectively – creating the perfect headspace for writing about my passion for human-first AI.

I've been that person addicted to social media – but I'm not anymore. And I'm not just surviving; I'm thriving. I don't want AI to become a similar addiction that people sink themselves into. Just like social media is a tool for connection, AI should be seen as a tool for support. As leaders, we need to keep our heads screwed on and not allow the bots to take over humanity.

Please continue making the decision to put the humans first.

P.S. I've enjoyed connecting with real-life humans throughout this process, and I look forward to connecting with more real-life humans via this book. If you enjoyed *AI-Human Fusion*, please leave a review on Amazon, Goodreads and/or Google (under HumanEdge AI Training). Your feedback means a lot!

About the Author

Leanne Shelton is the CEO and Founder of HumanEdge AI Training. In this role, she undertakes global AI coaching, keynote speaking, and training across all levels of business. Since 2023, she has been featured in *The Australian*, *ABC News*, *The CEO Magazine*, 6PR Perth radio and dozens of podcasts, industry journals and online publications.

Leanne graduated from Macquarie University with a Bachelor of Creative Arts (majoring in Creative Writing) before undertaking Marketing, PR, and Training and Assessment certifications through TAFE NSW.

After several years in marketing executive roles, 2014 saw Leanne launch her own marketing, SEO and copywriting agency: Write Time Marketing. After a decade of successful operation, she faced a professional crossroads due to the combined impact of post-COVID-19 economic downturns and the public launch of ChatGPT.

Leanne decided to turn her attention to coaching entrepreneurs (like her), teams and leaders, and groups in ethical, human-first AI adoption and use. After nearly two decades of marketing and training experience across numerous industries, this was a natural transition, which culminated in the founding of HumanEdge

AI Training. Her people-oriented, non-techy approach centred on human-based expertise has quickly become a point of difference in a tech- and IT-heavy industry that leaves otherwise keen adopters overwhelmed and in the dark.

The Sydney-based entrepreneur is a sought-after keynote speaker for summits and conferences across Sydney, Australia and Southeast Asia. She's inspired, educated and entertained thousands of people from hundreds of businesses and organisations. She also services a highly engaged online community across numerous platforms.

Outside of work, Leanne is a newly converted running and gym enthusiast, lover of dance, daily meditator, occasional yogi, engrossed book and audiobook consumer (especially business, self-development and psychological thrillers), dedicated wife, and frazzled mum to two daughters.

Connect with Leanne

- Leanne Shelton
- humanedgeai.com

Acknowledgements

Even though I'm someone who constantly challenges herself, writing a book about AI – while the world is still in a complete tizzy over the topic – was next level, even for me. But, here we are. Becoming an author has been a challenging, rewarding, and deeply personal journey. I couldn't have done it alone – and I'm immensely grateful to those who've helped bring this book to life.

First, thank *you* for downloading or picking up a copy of *AI-Human Fusion*. Thanks for trusting me to be part of your AI discovery journey and being open to exploring the messy, magical fusion between humans and machines. This book wasn't written to add to the hype – it was written for people like you, who want to use AI without losing the spark that makes us human.

I'm incredibly thankful to my online community of cheerleaders (maybe that includes you?) and long-time supporters from various parts of my life. Your incredible support and unwavering encouragement has fuelled me to keep going in this evolving, unknowable, AI-infused world.

This especially applies to my amazing professional network, from where I sourced and engaged the brilliant subject matter experts and thought-leaders who shared their wisdom and musings for this book. I've never claimed to be an expert in all things AI, which is exactly why the idea for *Hear from the Humans* struck me – because the best insights come from real humans with real experiences. Whether you simply contributed a quote or co-wrote a chapter with me, you've helped develop depth to *AI-Human Fusion* that otherwise wouldn't have existed.

To all my beta readers, especially Margaret King, Sally Cameron, and Kerryn Powell – thank you so much for your tireless editing, feedback, and encouragement. Also thank you to my fellow budding authors, Fleur Marks and Kylie Paatsch, for sharing your chapter layout tips and tricks. Especially when my 'neurospicy' brain wanted to just write and overlook the essential foundations.

Thank you to everyone involved in the production and publishing process. To Lesley Williams, thanks for your support and believing in this project from day one – even though I'd never written a book before. Huge thanks to the rest of the Major Street Publishing team – Duncan Blachford, Will Allen, and Production Works – and sales team at Hachette, for ensuring a super smooth, stress-free process. To Erin Huckle from Chuckle Communications, thank you for your dedicated efforts with the PR side of things and helping me spread my human-first message far and wide.

A big shout out is also necessary to my mentors, Kate Toon and Janine Garner, who've continually encouraged me to write a book on AI – even when I doubted myself. I appreciate your ongoing support.

Now I need to say a massive thank you to Daniel Markos who enthusiastically embraced this project as my right-hand man, supporting me by brainstorming ideas, conducting research, providing initial edits, reminding me to breathe and celebrate milestones, collating the final manuscript with hours to spare on deadline day, and helping me execute my marketing plans. You've made the whole book-writing thing an enjoyable and positive experience. Thank you.

To my parents, Narelle and Garry Belinfante, in-laws, Leah and Leonard Shelton, siblings, and extended family – thank you for your love, encouragement, and gentle curiosity about *what on earth* I've been working on all this time. Thanks for listening to me go on (and on) about this book for months. Your support means a lot.

Last, but definitely not least – to my husband, Justin, thank you for your patience when the deadlines loomed and my stress levels boomed. I appreciate it – and we survived! To our daughters, Gabrielle and Indiana, thanks for providing comic relief, hugs, and space when needed. I'm always striving to be a role model for you both and make you proud. In this weird and wonderful world, I hope you grow up seeing AI as something to use thoughtfully, creatively, and for good. I love you all very much.

References

ADP Research Institute. (2025, January). People at work 2024: A global workforce view. https://www.adpresearch.com/wp-content/uploads/2024/04/People-at-Work-2024-A-Global-Workforce-View.pdf.

Anthony, T. (2025, February 14). AI-Human Fusion Information Gathering (L. Shelton, Interviewer)

Australian Bureau of Statistics. (2024, July 26). *National Study of Mental Health and Wellbeing*, 2020–2022. Retrieved December 21, 2024, from https://www.abs.gov.au/statistics/health/mental-health/national-study-mental-health-and-wellbeing/latest-release

BluePatent. (2019). *Top inventions that nobody believed in*. Blue Patent. https://www.bluepatent.com/en/top-inventions-that-nobody-believed-in

CNN. (2024, May 16). *Hong Kong company loses $25 million in deepfake scam*. https://edition.cnn.com/2024/05/16/tech/arup-deepfake-scam-loss-hong-kong-intl-hnk/index.html

Dentons. (2024, April 26). *The current state of play for the regulation of AI in Australia in 2024*. https://www.dentons.com/en/insights/articles/2024/april/26/the-current-state-of-play-for-the-regulation-of-ai-in-australia-in-2024

Furrier, J. (2024, October 17). *IBM's "AI First" strategy: Redefining business with generative AI, quantum computing, and a culture of collaboration*. theCUBE Research. https://thecuberesearch.com/ibms-ai-first-strategy-redefining-business-with-generative-ai-quantum-computing-and-a-culture-of-collaboration/

Gartner, Inc. (2024). *Top 5 HR trends and priorities that matter most in 2025.* https://www.gartner.com/en/human-resources/trends/top-priorities-for-hr-leaders

Gartner Peer Community. (2023). *2024 generative AI planning: How are IT organizations preparing?* https://static.pulse.qa/omirs/2024-generative-ai-planning-how-it-organizations-preparing-zxm.pdf

Google Arts & Culture. (n.d.). *The everyday inventions people never thought would catch on.* https://artsandculture.google.com/story/the-everyday-inventions-people-never-thought-would-catch-on/LAVx2GNl1ScYLQ

Gosline, R. R. (2022, June 9). *Why AI customer journeys need more friction.* Harvard Business Review. https://hbr.org/2022/06/why-ai-customer-journeys-need-more-friction

Gupta, P. (2025, February 24). AI-Human Fusion Information Gathering (L. Shelton, Interviewer)

Hunter, N. (2023, January)*The Art of Prompt Engineering with ChatGPT.*

Kam, T. (2024, July 11). AI-Human Fusion Chapter Collaboration Discussion (L. Shelton, Interviewer)

Korshunov, P., & Marcel, S. (2020). Deepfake detection: humans vs. machines. arXiv preprint arXiv:2009.03155.

Mayer, H., Yee, L., Chiu, M., & Roberts, R. (2025). *Superagency in the Workplace: Empowering people to unlock AI's full potential.* McKinsey and Company.

Mariadassou, S., Klesse, A. K., & Boegershausen, J. (2024). Averse to what: Consumer aversion to algorithmic labels, but not their outputs?. *Current Opinion in Psychology,* 101839.

Medianet. (2024, October). *Fresh research reveals Australian workers have the highest stress levels in APAC.* https://newshub.medianet.com.au/2024/10/fresh-research-reveals-australian-workers-have-the-highest-stress-levels-in-apac/73253/

Miklos-Woodley, N., & Medling, V. *Healthy Hustle: The New Blueprint to Thrive in Business and in Life, Business Together Global* (2024).

References

Miklos-Woodley, N., & Medling, V. (2025, January 14). AI-Human Fusion Chapter Collaboration Discussion (L. Shelton, Interviewer)

Niu, B., & Mvondo, G. F. N. (2024). I Am ChatGPT, the ultimate AI Chatbot! Investigating the determinants of users' loyalty and ethical usage concerns of ChatGPT. *Journal of Retailing and Consumer Services, 76*, 103562.

Pijselman, M., & Litvinets, V. (2024, November 14). AI and Sustainability: Opportunities, challenges, and impact. EY. https://www.ey.com/en_nl/insights/climate-change-sustainability-services/ai-and-sustainability-opportunities-challenges-and-impact

Randstad. (2024, November). *Understanding talent scarcity: AI equity.* https://www.randstad.com/s3fs-media/rscom/public/2024-11/Randstad_understanding_talent_scarcity_AI_equity.pdf

Salesforce. (2024, August). *Unleashing an AI revolution: Inside Salesforce's decade-long journey.* https://www.salesforce.com/news/stories/ai-history-salesforce/

Salesforce. (2024, September). *How to provide AI-first service in 2025* [Video]. Salesforce+. https://www.salesforce.com/plus/specials/how-to-provide-ai-first-service-in-2025

Sandoval, E. (2024, November). *Should you be polite to artificial intelligence?* UNSW Sydney. https://www.unsw.edu.au/newsroom/news/2024/11/should-you-be-polite-to-artificial-intelligence

Schneier, B. (2024, May). *LLMs, data control, and path insecurity.* Schneier on Security. https://www.schneier.com/blog/archives/2024/05/llms-data-control-path-insecurity.html

Suresh, N. (2025, February 10). AI-Human Fusion Chapter Collaboration Discussion (L. Shelton, Interviewer)

Tortoise Media. (2024, September 18). *The Global Artificial Intelligence Index 2024.* https://www.tortoisemedia.com/2024/09/18/the-global-artificial-intelligence-index-2024

UNEP. (2024, February). *AI has an environmental problem. Here's what the world can do about it.* https://www.unep.org/news-and-stories/story/ai-has-environmental-problem-heres-what-world-can-do-about

Vox. (2015, February 9). *7 world-changing inventions people thought were dumb fads.* https://www.vox.com/2015/2/9/8004661/fads-inventions-changed-world

World Intellectual Property Organization. (2020). *What is intellectual property?* https://www.wipo.int/edocs/pubdocs/en/wipo_pub_450_2020.pdf

Zhang, Y., & Gosline, R. (2023). *Human favoritism, not AI aversion: People's perceptions (and bias) toward generative AI, human experts, and human–GAI collaboration in persuasive content generation.* Judgment and Decision Making, 18, e41.1